Sugar-free
diet

igloobooks

igloobooks

Published in 2015
by Igloo Books Ltd
Cottage Farm
Sywell
NN6 0BJ
www.igloobooks.com

FIR003 0215
2 4 6 8 10 9 7 5 3 1
ISBN 978-1-78440-137-5

Printed and manufactured in China

Contents

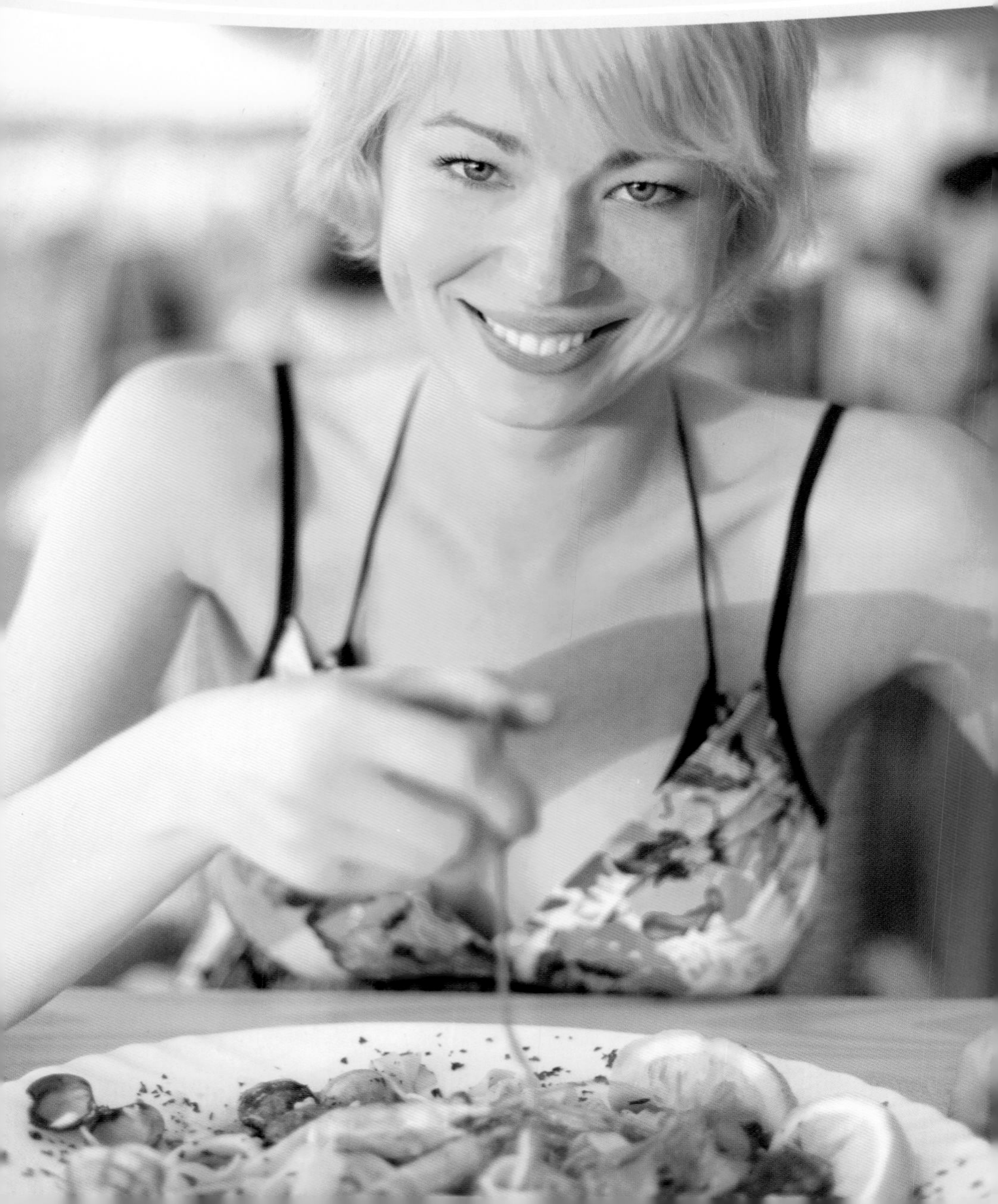

Introduction

You've probably heard a lot about sugar in the news recently. Obesity is on the rise, along with diabetes, heart disease and a host of other health problems. Many of these problems are being blamed on eating too much sugar. You may think that you keep your sugar intake under control, but many of us do not realise just how much sugar is hidden in the food we eat.

A growing problem

For thousands of years, people ate very little sugar. Honey was used sparingly as a sweetener.

However, in the last couple of centuries, as refined sugar has become cheaper and more readily available, our sugar intake has massively increased. Now, many people with busy lives rely on processed food for convenience, and many of these are loaded with hidden sugar.

What to do?

If you go online, you will find a lot of conflicting advice. It can be hard to make sense of all the different opinions out there. The one thing that most experts agree on is that too much sugar is bad for you. Cutting down on the amount of sugar you eat is certainly not going to hurt you – in fact, it could help you improve your overall health.

Many people are choosing to take the plunge and cut sugar from their diet. Some try to eliminate sugar completely; others do their best to get their intake within recommended guidelines. Most people who cut down on sugar say that they feel better and look great as a result. Why not try it for yourself?

Why Cut Out Sugar?

There are a lot of compelling reasons for cutting sugar from your diet: to improve your overall health, to lose weight or even to reduce the risk of serious illnesses. Most of us eat more sugar than we should, but not everyone realises the consequences this has on our bodies.

Many foods that contain added sugar have a lot of calories with few other nutrients. Eating too much of these foods can make you overweight, which can lead to a whole host of health problems. One study found that a person's risk of dying from heart disease rose along with the percentage of sugar in their diet – no matter how young or active they were. Diabetes is the other big risk associated with eating too much sugar. Our bodies produce insulin to help break down sugar. A person with diabetes cannot produce enough insulin to cope with the sugar they eat. Left untreated, diabetes can cause complications such as stroke, nerve damage, blindness and kidney disease.

Take care of your teeth

Sugary foods and drinks are a major cause of tooth decay. Your mouth is naturally full of bacteria and when you 'feed' the bacteria with sugary foods and drinks, they break down the sugars and produce acid. This acid can decay the surface of your teeth, causing cavities. Brushing regularly will help prevent this, but it is also important to limit your sugar intake.

Do we need sugar?

Calories are a measure of the energy a food contains. Sugar provides energy that we need, but it is only one source of energy. We should aim to get most of our calories from other kinds of food, such as lean proteins, starchy foods and fresh fruits and vegetables.

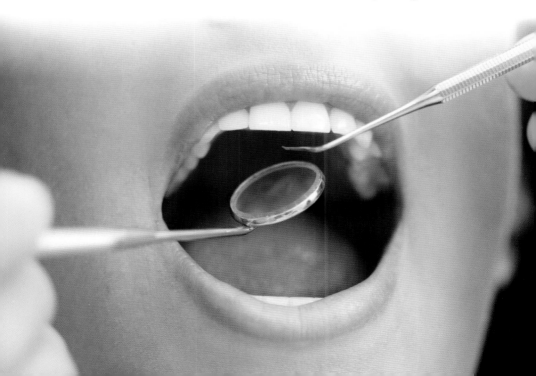

Types of Sugar

When you think of sugar, you probably think of white granulated sugar, but sugar comes in many forms. Some types are found naturally in foods, while others are added during cooking or processing.

Most of the sugar that we add to our food is sucrose, which comes from either sugar cane or sugar beets. The juice is extracted from the plants and impurities are removed. Then the juice is crystallised into what we call 'refined sugar'. Whether it comes from sugar cane or sugar beets, the end product is identical. Demerara sugar and brown sugar are made using the same process. They are a bit less refined but just as full of empty calories.

Not created equally

The glycaemic index (GI) measures by how much, gram for gram, a substance raises your blood glucose level compared with glucose. Foods with a high glycaemic index, such as sucrose, are broken down quickly and release glucose rapidly into the bloodstream, giving you a 'sugar rush' that quickly fades. Foods with a low glycaemic index release glucose slowly, giving you energy over a longer period of time.

Natural sugars

Fruit contains a type of sugar called fructose. Fructose occurs naturally in the fruit and is not added. Fructose has a lower glycaemic index than sucrose, so it is safer for diabetics, but everyone should still limit the amount of fructose they eat.

Sugar substitutes

Scientists have developed a range of substances with the sweetness of sugar but fewer calories. If you love the taste of sweet things, these artificial sweeteners can deliver the taste of sugar with virtually no calories. They do not harm your teeth, and diabetics can eat them more safely than sugar. However, they are best eaten in moderation. Stevia, a sugar substitute from the stevia plant, is a natural product with many of the same benefits. Agave nectar, brown rice syrup and maple syrup are all examples of sugar substitutes that release energy more slowly than sugar.

How Much is Enough?

As scientists learn more about the effects of sugar on the body, the recommendations change. For many years the advice was to limit added sugars to ten per cent or lower of your calorie intake. This works out at about 70 grams (2 ½ oz) per day for men and 50 grams (1 ⁴/₅ oz) for women, though it varies depending on your weight and how active you are.

To put it into perspective, one teaspoon of sugar is about 4 grams (¹/₅ oz), so the average woman is recommended to have no more than 12 teaspoons of sugar a day. That may sound like a lot, but a regular-sized can of soft drink has about nine teaspoons of sugar, and some chocolate bars have in excess of eight teaspoons. Add a yoghurt or a bowl of breakfast cereal and you can use up your daily allowance before you realise it.

Going lower

The World Health Organization (WHO) has recently published new recommendations calling for adults to cut their sugar intake in half – to about six teaspoons a day. To achieve this, you will have to be really smart about what you eat. Natural sugars, such as those found in fruit, are not included in the six teaspoons but many types of processed food have added sugar. For example, a tablespoon of tomato ketchup can contain a teaspoon of sugar.

Taking the right steps

To cut added sugars from your diet you will have to be disciplined. Reading food labels carefully is a huge part of this, and reducing your intake of processed foods is another key step. If you make your meals yourself from fresh ingredients, you will know exactly what goes in them.

Going Sugar Free

So you have had a look at the evidence and decided to cut sugar from your diet. Congratulations! It won't always be easy, but people all over the world are already seeing the benefits of reduced sugar intake – and now you can join them.

Keep a diary

You may think that your sugar intake is fairly low, but most of us eat more sugar than we realise. Keep a detailed food diary for a few days, recording everything you eat and drink. Check labels carefully to work out your total sugar intake. That will give you a good starting point for setting targets when you start to go sugar free.

How low can you go?

If you search online, you will find many different approaches to going sugar free. Many people focus on eliminating added sugar from their diet. Others take it a step further and eliminate all foods containing sugar, even natural sugars such as those found in fruit. How far you want to go is up to you. Your body doesn't need sugar, so it won't be harmed by eliminating it completely. However, fruits have a lot of other nutrients that are good for you. Most doctors recommend limiting the amount of fruit you eat, but not cutting it out entirely.

Cutting sugar out of your diet is definitely a challenge, but it does not have to be an all-or-nothing exercise. If you reduce your sugar intake slowly, while still allowing yourself a few occasional treats, you will still feel some of the health benefits. Once you start cutting out sugar, you will soon get used to it and be able to cut out even more. The lower you go, the better you will feel.

Take it slow

If you are used to having sugar in your diet, suddenly cutting it out entirely will be a shock to the system. You might manage a few days of the new regime and then give up. It is much more effective to reduce your sugar intake gradually, over a few weeks or months. This gives your body a chance to adjust to the new diet. For example, you can start to reduce the amount of sugar you put in tea or coffee, or cut down on the number of fizzy drinks you have. Once that feels 'normal', you can reduce it further.

You may feel tired at first when you start cutting out sugar. Some people experience headaches and cravings for sweet things. Make sure you are eating a healthy, balanced diet and try a piece of fruit to fend off sugar cravings. Soon your body will be used to it and you will feel great.

Feeling good

Once you are used to having less sugar, you will start to feel – and see – changes in your body. Many people who go sugar-free report that they feel less hungry and have more energy. This is because your body uses up sugar quickly but energy from other sources, such as vegetables, is much longer-lasting. You will probably also start to lose weight.

Keep it simple

At first, going sugar free will take up time. You will be spending more time reading labels, planning meals and trying new recipes. If you try to do it at the same time as taking on a big project at work, or planning a holiday or wedding, for example, you might feel overwhelmed. Choose a time when you can focus on your diet without too many distractions. Once you are into the swing of it, things will go back to normal.

Reading Food Labels

Sometimes it is not obvious how much sugar a particular food contains. If you want to cut out sugar, you will need to read nutrition labels carefully. Have a look at the labels on the foods in your cupboards and your fridge – you will probably be amazed at how much sugar some of them have.

What to look for

Nutrition labels show the amount of sugar per 100 g (3 ½ oz) of food, which makes it easy to compare different foods. Find the figure for 'Carbohydrates (of which sugars)' on the label. If the figure is more than 22.5 g (¾ oz) of total sugars per 100 g (3 ½ oz), that is considered to be a high amount of sugar. Anything with 5 g or fewer per 100 g (3 ½ oz) is low sugar.

These figures include natural sugars, such as those found in fruit and milk, as well as added sugars. If you have two foods that have the same total amount of sugar, but one is high in milk and fruit, it is a better choice.

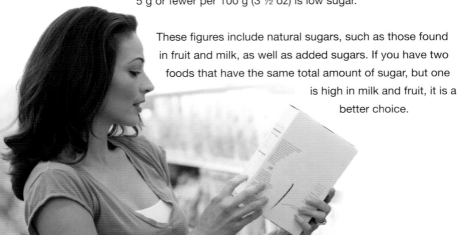

Traffic lights

Some foods have labels on the front of the packaging that show you at a glance whether they are high in sugar. They usually use a traffic-light system: red for high, amber for medium and green for low. If you're rushing to finish your shop and don't have time to read the ingredients lists, ditch the red foods and make sure that your basket is filled with green ones.

It doesn't take an expert to realise that foods such as sweets, biscuits, cakes and chocolate contain a lot of sugar. However, many other packaged foods can have surprisingly high amounts of added sugar too. Reading labels carefully will help you cut out added sugars from your diet.

Sugar by a different name

All packaged foods are required to list their ingredients by order of weight, so the first names on the list make up the bulk of the food. Added sugars can sometimes be camouflaged when they appear in ingredients lists. Here are some other terms you might see:

sucrose • glucose • maltose • barley malt • hydrolysed starch
• inverted sugar syrup • fruit juice concentrate • corn syrup • honey

These are all types of added sugar. If you find them near the top of the ingredients list, stay away.

What Not to Eat

Steering clear of chocolate breakfast cereals is a no-brainer, but even some of the seemingly healthier brands can have a lot of added sugar. Don't be fooled by packets that say 'reduced sugar', 'enriched' or 'wholegrain' – these labels can make a product look healthy but the nutrition label will tell you the truth. Some foods, such as yoghurts, that are advertised as 'fat-free' often have a lot of sugar added to make up for the taste lost when fat is removed.

Make your own

Have you ever made your own pasta sauce? Now is a great time to start! Jars of pasta sauce often contain a lot of added sugar, but if you make your own you will know it is sugar free. It is easier than you might think, and you can make a big batch and freeze portions for another day.

Drinks

Fizzy drinks are one of the biggest no-nos if you want to go sugar free. A single can of soft drink can contain more than half the recommended daily limit of sugar. Diet soft drinks are lower in sugar but have no real nutritional value. If you cannot survive without fizzy drinks, try diluting unsweetened fruit juice with sparkling water. But watch out for juice drinks that are sweetened with added sugar!

Alcoholic drinks contain sugar but some are better than others. For example, a dry red wine has less sugar than white wine. You should avoid champagne and sweet dessert wines. Spirits such as gin, vodka and whisky are low in sugar, but be careful of mixers – they are usually full of sugar. Stick to soda water, diet or slimline mixers, or drink it neat.

Low-sugar Stars

It is easy to look at a list of high-sugar foods and wonder what is left that is 'safe' to eat. Luckily, there is a huge range of low-sugar foods available. Even a picky eater will find plenty of healthy foods to from which to choose.

Meat and fish

Lean meats and fish are a great low-sugar option because they are packed with protein and other nutrients. Watch out for sugar-cured meats, such as some types of ham, and sauces or marinades that might be high in sugar. Eggs, beans and unsalted nuts are also good sources of low-sugar protein.

Go green

Vegetables are one of the best options for a sugar-free diet because most are very low in natural sugars. A few to watch out for are beetroot, carrot and parsnip, which contain a higher amount of natural sugar. You can still eat them, just in moderation. Broccoli, asparagus, beans and sweet potatoes are full of nutrients and low in sugar.

Grains

Carbohydrates are found in grains such as wheat. Your body turns carbohydrates into sugars, so many people on a sugar-free diet try to limit the carbohydrates they consume. As a general rule, stay away from refined white flour and foods made from it, such as white bread and pasta. Other grains, such as oats and brown rice, are much healthier. When choosing bread products, look out for 'wholegrain' on the label and make sure to check for added sugar.

Breakfast

When it comes to breakfast, plain porridge is a low-sugar winner but if you prefer toast, you can still eat it. Make sure to choose wholegrain bread and replace jam or chocolate spreads with cream cheese.

Fruit: Friend or Foe?

One of the main topics of debate among people going sugar free is whether or not to eat fruit. Fruit contains fructose, a type of natural sugar, so many people eliminate it from their diets along with refined and added sugars. However, it is not so simple. Unlike refined sugar, fruits contain a lot of useful nutrients including fibre, vitamin C, folic acid and potassium.

Many doctors and nutritionists recommend keeping fruit in your diet but limiting the quantity you eat – two pieces a day is a common guideline. Vegetables have many of the same nutrients as fruits but fewer calories and less sugar, so replace fruits with vegetables wherever you can. When you eat fruit, make sure it is as low-sugar as possible. For example, choose tins of fruit in juice rather than in syrup.

The best fruits

In nutritional terms, no two fruits are alike. Some have more fructose and fibre than others. As a general rule, you should avoid fruits that have a high fructose content but little fibre, and try to eat those with high fibre and low fructose.

Instead of...	Eat
Grapes	Raspberries
Apple	Pear
Banana	Kiwi fruit
Cherries	Cranberries
Watermelon	Blueberries

No juice!

Sugars in fruits are less likely to cause tooth decay because of the way the sugars are contained within the structure of the fruit. When fruit is turned into juice, the sugars are released, so it's best to cut out fruit juice and stick to eating whole fruit and drinking water instead.

Eating Out

Eating a meal at a restaurant with friends is one of life's great joys, but you don't always know exactly what goes into the food. How can you stick to a sugar-free diet while eating out? It definitely takes more willpower than eating at home. Here are a few tips to help you:

- Arrive with a positive mindset – be excited about what you *can* eat rather than focusing on what you can't

- Order a starter and a main meal rather than a main meal and a dessert

- Stick to fish, meat and vegetables when choosing your food

Be prepared

If you are going to eat out, you might be able to plan ahead. Some restaurants have nutritional information for their menus posted on their websites. Have a look before you go out and choose an option that is sugar free, or at least low in sugar.

- Go easy on condiments and salad dressings – these often have a lot of sugar. A plain vinaigrette dressing is usually low in sugar but watch out for balsamic vinegar, which is high is sugar

- Avoid dishes with tomato-based or fruity sauces

- Ask the waiter about the menu – because many people are choosing to go sugar free, restaurants are used to being asked which dishes are lowest in sugar

- Don't be afraid to order your food exactly as you want it. If there is a sauce that might be sugary, ask to have it left off your plate

- Go for sparkling water rather than a fizzy drink. If you want alcohol, choose a small glass of dry red wine

- If your friends try to tempt you into eating a sugary treat, be firm and explain how much better you are feeling as a result of your new diet

Being Active, Staying Safe

Going sugar free is just one part of a new, healthier lifestyle. If you seriously reduce your sugar intake, you will probably lose weight, and if you increase the amount of exercise you do then you will lose even more. Being active does not have to mean joining a gym or doing a sport you hate – even small changes in your daily routine can have a positive impact.

You don't have to break a sweat to get the benefit from exercise. It's all about keeping moving throughout the day and you can work it into things you already do. Instead of using the lift, take the stairs. Walk about while you talk on the phone. Get off the bus two or three stops earlier and walk the rest of the way. If you are driving to the shops, park a bit further away than usual. Little things like this can really add up!

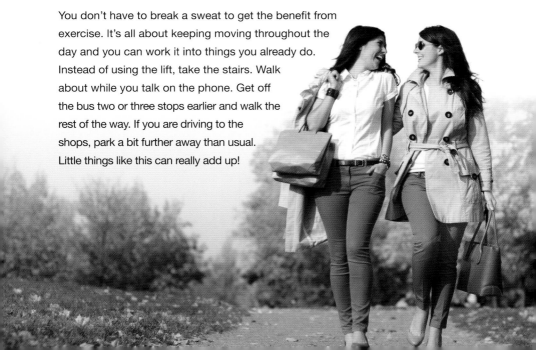

If you are ready to step it up a bit, jogging, cycling and swimming are great ways to burn calories. Don't worry if you are stuck indoors – put on some music and dance around the house or give the housework some extra oomph!

Feel the benefits

Keeping active is great for your health. It helps keep your heart healthy, reduces your risk of serious illness and strengthens muscles and bones. It can make you lose weight more quickly and often leaves you feeling more energetic.

Working together

Find a friend who is also trying to be more active. If you have someone to exercise with, you'll be more motivated to keep it up. Taking a short walk at lunch with a work colleague will burn calories – and it's a great excuse for a chat, too!

Is it safe?

Going sugar free is just like any other major lifestyle change – you should make sure you are ready for it. Even if you are in good health, it's best to talk to your doctor before you start. He or she can make sure your body can cope with a change in diet and maybe even provide some useful tips!

It is especially important to talk to your doctor if you are pregnant or trying to become pregnant, if you have a history of eating disorders or if you have any other health concerns. Your doctor might want to do a blood test for diabetes before you start, especially if you have a history of it in your family.

Ready to go

Before you start, have a look through your kitchen and get rid of anything that is going to tempt you. So often we eat things just because they are there, not because we are particularly hungry. If your cupboards are full of biscuits, it is going to be hard to stick to a sugar-free diet. Make a fresh start by filling your cupboards and fridge with healthy snacks such as nuts and carrot sticks.

Tell your friends and family about your new regime. If they know what you are doing, they can offer help and support – and they will not tempt you with offers of sweet treats. They might even want to join in! Any kind of lifestyle change is easier if you're not doing it alone.

Keep track

Before you start your sugar-free diet, step on the scales and take a photo of yourself so that you can make comparisons once you lose weight. Make a note of your measurements – sometimes it can feel like the weight loss is slow, but you'll probably be losing centimetres.

Keeping Motivated

Sticking to any kind of new routine is easiest if you have a clear idea why you are doing it. You also have to know what you want to get out of it. Sit down and make a list of your reasons for going sugar free. If you hang it somewhere visible, then you can look at it any time you feel like you can't do it. Reminding yourself of all those health benefits can give you the motivation to keep going.

Make a plan

Think about how you want to cut down your sugar intake. If you are doing it gradually rather than cold turkey, write down a plan to show your targets, week by week. You might even choose some low-sugar recipes to try each week. It is easy to get so busy that you just want to make things easier by going back to your old routine. If you already have a plan in place, you'll be more likely to stick with it.

Setting goals

What do you hope to get out of going sugar free? Most people want to improve their health and lose weight. Think about your short-term and long-term goals. Set yourself a realistic target weight and make a plan for how to get there.

Support from friends

Share your plans and goals with a close friend. He or she can help you keep track of your progress and offer encouragement and support – as well as a big hug when you reach your goals!

Reward yourself

Set up a star chart for yourself. It works for children, so why not for you? Every day that you stick to your sugar limits, give yourself a star. Once you have enough stars you can reward yourself with a prize, such as a magazine or a new item of clothing.

Breakfast

A healthy, sugar-free breakfast can provide long-lasting energy that will keep you from snacking later in the morning.

From breakfast cereal to sweetened tea, it is easy to let the sugar add up when having breakfast. Make sure to read the labels and know exactly what you are eating – for example, many breakfast cereals have a lot of added sugar. Wholegrain options, such as plain shredded wheat, are good choices. Muesli may seem like a healthy option but some shop-bought varieties are loaded with sugar. If you prefer toast, use wholegrain bread and a savoury spread such as low-fat cream cheese or avocado. A vegetable omelette is quick to prepare and full of nutrients. Scrambled eggs with smoked salmon provide protein that will keep you going until lunchtime.

If you really need a hit of sweetness to get you going in the morning, do it the healthy way, by adding a handful of fresh berries to whatever you are eating.

Green Omelette with Salmon

Serves: **4** | Preparation time: **10–15 minutes**

Cooking time: **6–8 minutes**

Ingredients

- 8 large eggs, separated
- 110 ml / 4 fl. oz / ½ cup fat-free milk
- 55 g / 2 oz / ⅓ cup buckwheat flour
- a large handful of cress, washed and dried
- 1 tbsp unsalted butter
- 75 g / 3 oz / ½ cup smoked salmon slices
- 2 tbsp low-fat plain yoghurt, to serve
- salt and freshly ground black pepper

Method

1. Preheat the oven to 180°C (160°C fan) / 350F / gas 4.

2. Combine 8 egg yolks and 6 whites in a food processor with the milk, flour, most of the cress and some seasoning. Blitz until smooth, then pour into a bowl.

3. Briefly whisk the remaining egg whites with a pinch of salt until softly peaked, then fold into the batter.

4. Heat the butter in a large, heatproof non-stick frying pan set over a moderate heat.

5. Add the batter and let it set for 2 minutes. Transfer the pan to the oven to finish cooking for 6–8 minutes. Remove from the oven and leave to cool slightly, then turn out and slice.

6. Serve on plates with the remaining cress, smoked salmon and a little plain yoghurt.

Muesli with Raspberries

Serves: **4** | Preparation time: **5 minutes**
Cooking time: **5 minutes**

Ingredients

- 300 g / 10 ½ oz / 2 cups rolled oats
- 55 g / 2 oz / ⅓ cup raisins
- 2 tbsp walnuts
- 75 g / 3 oz / ½ cup dried apricots, chopped
- 110 g / 4 oz / ⅔ cup raspberries
- 110 g / 4 oz / ½ cup plain yoghurt

Method

1. Mix together the oats, raisins and walnuts in a large mixing bowl.
2. Divide between cereal bowls and top with the apricots, raspberries and a generous dollop of yoghurt.
3. Serve immediately.

Apple and Walnut Porridge

Serves: **4** | Preparation time: **5 minutes**
Cooking time: **6–7 minutes**

Ingredients

- 150 g / 5 oz / 1 ½ cups rolled oats
- 450 ml / 16 fl. oz / 2 cups semi-skimmed milk
- 375 ml / 13 fl. oz / 1 ½ cups cold water
- 2 small gala or Fuji apples, cored and chopped
- 55 g / 2 oz / ½ cup walnuts, crushed
- 2 tsp ground cinnamon

Method

1. Combine the oats, milk and water in a large, heavy-based saucepan set over a medium heat.

2. Bring the liquid to a simmer and cook steadily for 6–7 minutes, stirring frequently, until thickened and creamy.

3. Spoon into bowls and top with chopped apple, crushed walnuts and a sprinkling of ground cinnamon before serving.

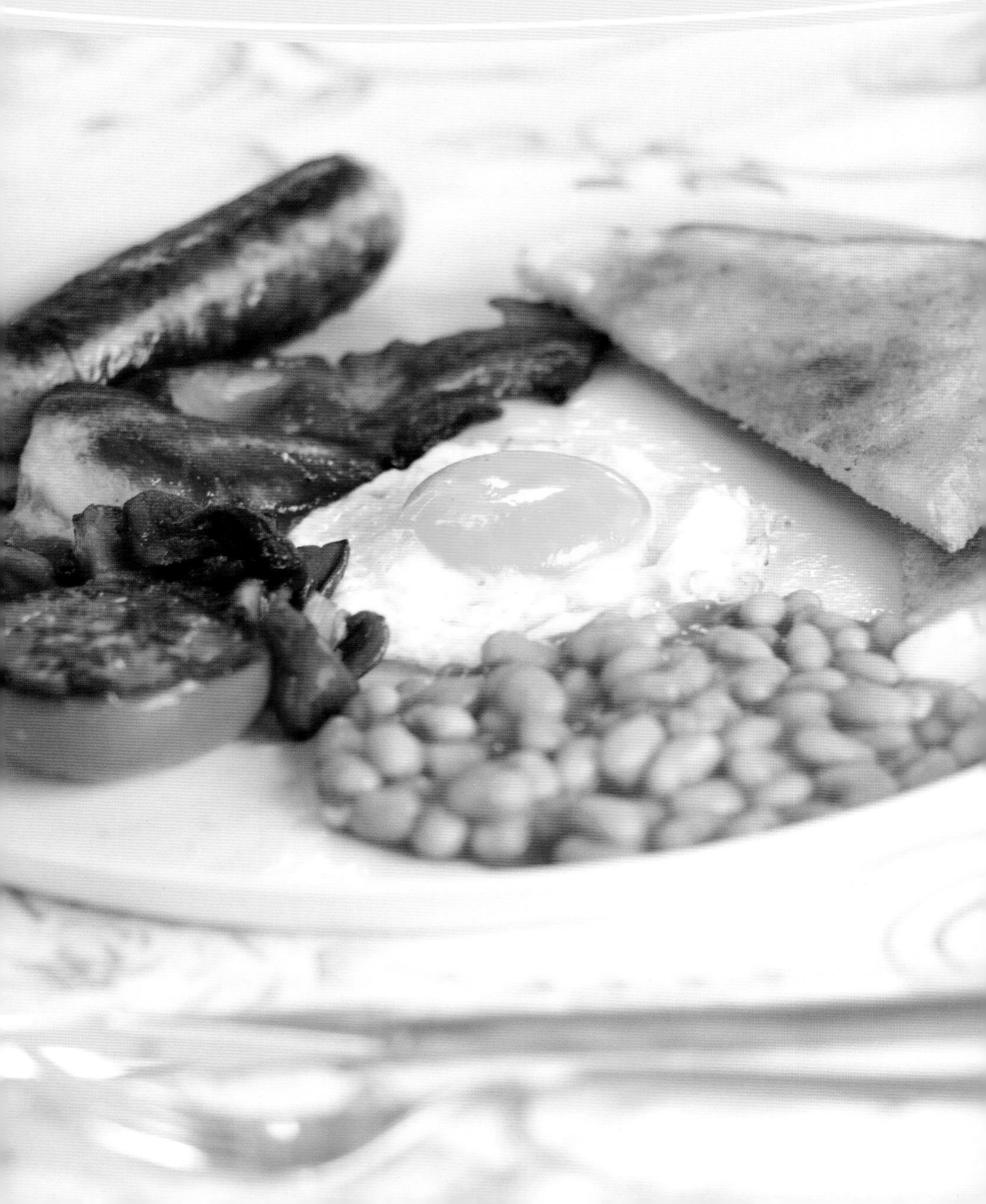

English Breakfast

Serves: **4** | Preparation time: **5 minutes**
Cooking time: **10–15 minutes**

Ingredients

- 75 ml / 3 fl. oz / ⅓ cup hot water
- 1 ½ tbsp tomato purée
- 1 tsp Worcestershire sauce
- 300 g / 10 ½ oz / 1 ½ cups canned white haricot beans, drained
- 4 rashers of back bacon
- 4 pork sausages
- 2 medium salad tomatoes, halved horizontally
- 1 tbsp unsalted butter
- 100 g / 3 ½ oz / 1 ½ cups button mushrooms, chopped
- 1 tbsp sunflower oil
- medium eggs
- 4 slices of white sandwich bread
- salt and freshly ground black pepper

Method

1. Preheat the grill to hot. Whisk together the hot water, tomato purée, Worcestershire sauce and seasoning in a pan. Add the beans and cook over a low heat, stirring, until soft. Season to taste.

2. Arrange the bacon, sausages and halved tomatoes on a grilling tray. Season the tomatoes. Grill the bacon and tomatoes for 2–3 minutes on both sides, then remove from the tray. Grill the sausages for a further 3–4 minutes, turning occasionally, until cooked through.

3. Meanwhile, melt the butter in a frying pan set over a moderate heat. Sauté the mushrooms for 3–4 minutes, with seasoning, until golden. Remove from the pan, wipe clean, and add the oil.

4. Fry the eggs until the white and yolks are set. Toast the slices of bread under the grill or in a toaster until golden; cut in half diagonally and serve with the rest of the cooked breakfast.

Coddled Egg with Ham

Serves: **4** | Preparation time: **5–10 minutes**
Cooking time: **3–4 minutes**

Ingredients

- 2 tbsp olive oil
- 4 slices of prosciutto
- 75 g / 3 oz / ½ cup cherry tomatoes, halved
- 4 large eggs
- 2 tbsp Parmesan, finely grated
- 2 tbsp balsamic vinegar
- a few sprigs of thyme
- salt and freshly ground black pepper

Method

1. Grease four individual ramekins with the olive oil.
2. Line with the prosciutto and cherry tomatoes, then crack in the eggs.
3. Top with Parmesan, balsamic vinegar, thyme and seasoning, then sit in a large saucepan.
4. Fill the saucepan with boiling water so that it reaches halfway up the sides of the ramekins. Place the saucepan over a medium heat and cover with a lid.
5. Leave the eggs to cook for 3–4 minutes until set.
6. Once set, carefully remove from the saucepan before serving.

Green Tea Bagels

Serves: **4** | Preparation time: **1 hour 5–10 minutes**

Cooking time: **20 minutes**

Ingredients

- 200 g / 7 oz / 1 ⅓ cups strong white bread flour, plus extra for dusting
- 100 ml / 3 ½ fl. oz / ½ cup cold water
- 2 tsp matcha green tea powder
- 1 ½ tsp salt
- ¾ tsp dried fast-action yeast

Method

1. Combine the flour, water, matcha powder, salt and yeast, and mix well until a dough forms. Turn out onto a floured surface and knead for 10–12 minutes. Divide the dough into four pieces and roll into balls. Cover loosely with oiled cling film and leave to rest for 15 minutes.

2. Roll out each piece into a 15 cm x 8 cm (6 in x 3 in) oval on a floured surface, then shape into a thick sausage, roughly 3–4 cm (1 ½ in) wide.

3. Join both ends to make rough doughnut shapes. Seal well and leave to rest in a warm place for 30 minutes as you preheat the oven to 180°C (160°C fan) / 350F / gas 4.

4. Bring a saucepan of water to the boil and drop in the bagels. Cook for 30 seconds, flip and cook the other sides for 30 seconds.

5. Remove and pat dry, then bake for 20 minutes. Allow to cool before serving.

Blueberry Muesli

Serves: **4–6** | Preparation time: **5 minutes**
Cooking time: **5 minutes**

Ingredients

- 350 g / 12 oz / 2 ⅓ cups rolled oats
- 75 g / 3 oz / ½ cup sultanas
- 2 tbsp raisins
- 2 tbsp golden sultanas
- 2 tbsp dried banana chips
- 450 g / 1 lb / 2 cups low-fat yoghurt
- 100 g / 3 ½ oz / ⅔ cup blueberries

Method

1. Heat a large frying pan over a medium heat until hot.

2. Add the oats and dry fry for 30–40 seconds until they start to toast and become fragrant.

3. Pour into a large mixing bowl and add the sultanas, raisins, golden sultanas and banana chips.

4. Stir well. The muesli can now be stored in airtight container.

5. To serve, spoon some muesli into serving bowls and top with yoghurt.

6. Sprinkle over a little more muesli before topping with blueberries and serving.

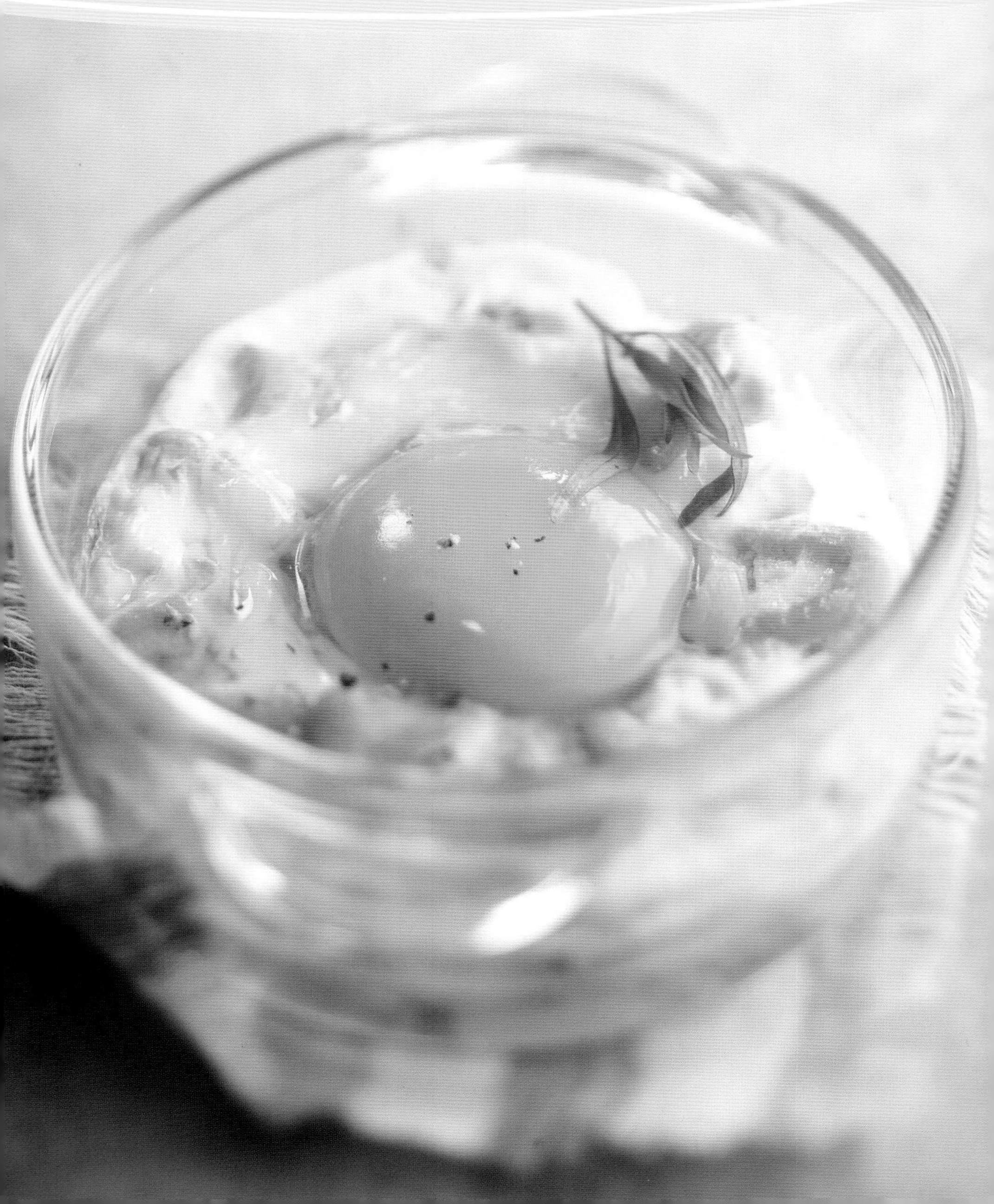

Coddled Egg with Salmon

Serves: **4** | Preparation time: **5 minutes**
Cooking time: **3–4 minutes**

Ingredients

- 1 tbsp unsalted butter
- 100 g / 3 ½ oz / ⅔ cup smoked salmon trimmings
- 4 large eggs
- a few sprigs of tarragon, to garnish
- salt and freshly ground black pepper

Method

1. Grease four glass ramekins with the butter.

2. Arrange the smoked salmon trimmings in each ramekin, then crack one egg into each ramekin.

3. Season and arrange the ramekins in a large, heavy-based saucepan or casserole dish.

4. Pour in enough boiling water around the ramekins to reach halfway up them.

5. Cover the saucepan with a lid and cook over a low heat for 3–4 minutes until the eggs are set.

6. Remove from the saucepan and serve immediately with a sprig of tarragon on top as a garnish.

Soft-boiled Egg with Asparagus

Serves: **4** | Preparation time: **10–15 minutes**

Cooking time: **10 minutes**

Ingredients

- 6 small eggs
- 50 g / 2 oz / ⅓ cup plain (all-purpose) flour
- 150 g / 5 oz / 1 cup panko breadcrumbs
- 55 ml / 2 fl. oz / ¼ cup sunflower oil
- salt and freshly ground black pepper

Method

1. Bring a saucepan of salted water to the boil, and blanch the asparagus for 2 minutes.

2. Drain well and pat dry, then leave to cool.

3. Boil four of the eggs for 8 minutes. Remove and run under cold, running water for 1 minute and leave to cool to one side.

4. Season the flour and whisk the remaining eggs in a bowl with some seasoning.

5. Dust the asparagus in flour, shaking off any excess, then dip in the egg to coat. Roll in the breadcrumbs and place on a lined plate.

6. Heat the oil in a wide-rimmed frying or sauté pan until hot.

7. Shallow-fry the asparagus spears until golden and crisp on the outside. Drain, then serve alongside the soft-boiled eggs in cups.

Stack of Pancakes

Serves: **4–6** | Preparation time: **5–10 minutes**
Cooking time: **15 minutes**

Ingredients

- 200 g / 7 oz / 1 ⅓ cups plain (all-purpose) flour
- 2 tsp baking powder
- a pinch of salt
- 2 large eggs, beaten
- 3 tbsp unsalted butter, melted
- 250 ml / 9 fl. oz / 1 cup semi-skimmed milk
- 1 tbsp cumin seeds, to garnish

Method

1. Sift the flour into a large mixing bowl and stir through the baking powder and salt.

2. Combine the eggs with one tablespoon of the melted butter and the milk, then add to the dry ingredients and whisk well until you have a smooth batter.

3. Add a little of the remaining melted butter to a non-stick frying pan and cook small ladles of the batter until set and blistered on top.

4. Flip and cook the other sides for a further minute until set and golden.

5. Repeat this method, using a little melted butter each time, until you have used up the batter.

6. Stack the pancakes and garnish with cumin seeds on top before serving.

Buckwheat Crêpes

Serves: **4** | Preparation time: **15 minutes**

Cooking time: **20 minutes**

Ingredients

- 3 tbsp unsalted butter, melted
- 150 g / 5 oz / 2 cups button mushrooms, finely chopped
- 125 g / 4 ½ oz / ¾ cup buckwheat flour
- 5 medium eggs
- 250 ml / 9 fl. oz / 1 cup water
- 1 tbsp sunflower oil
- a small bunch of chives, snipped
- salt and freshly ground black pepper

Method

1. Add a tablespoon of melted butter to a sauté pan set over a moderate heat. Add the mushrooms and sauté with seasoning for 4–5 minutes, stirring until tender. Set to one side.

2. Mix the flour and a teaspoon of salt in a bowl. Crack in one egg and whisk, gradually adding water until you have a smooth batter.

3. Heat the melted butter in a large crêpe pan. Add a ladle of batter to coat the base. Once the top starts to blister, flip the crêpe and cook for 1 minute. Repeat until you have four large crêpes, then set to one side.

4. Heat the oil in a frying pan set over a moderate heat. Fry the remaining eggs until the whites and yolks are set. Spoon the mushrooms into the centre of the crêpes and fold the edges around. Serve immediately with the fried egg, chives and seasoning.

Egg with Turkey Bacon

Serves: **4** | Preparation time: **5 minutes**
Cooking time: **10 minutes**

Ingredients

- 4 medium eggs
- 1 tbsp white wine vinegar
- 1 tbsp sunflower oil
- 4 rashers of thick-cut turkey bacon
- 4 small slices of white sandwich bread
- a few sprigs of chervil, to garnish
- salt and freshly ground black pepper

Method

1. Bring a large saucepan of water to a simmer and stir through the white wine vinegar.

2. Crack the eggs into cups, then gently tip into the simmering water. Poach at a steady simmer for 3 minutes. Remove with a slotted spoon to kitchen paper to drain. Cover loosely with aluminium foil to keep warm.

3. Heat the oil in a large sauté pan set over a moderate heat until hot. Fry the turkey bacon for 2–3 minutes on both sides until golden brown and crisp at the edges. Drain on kitchen paper, then cut into strips.

4. Toast the slices of bread in a toaster until golden. Remove, cut off the crusts and cut into soldiers. Arrange the soldiers on plates and sit a poached egg on top.

5. Serve with the turkey bacon, a sprig of chervil and a little seasoning.

Scrambled Eggs

Serves: **4** | Preparation time: **5 minutes**

Cooking time: **10 minutes**

Ingredients

- 2 tbsp unsalted butter, cubed
- 150 g / 5 oz / 2 cups button mushrooms, sliced
- 6 large eggs
- 75 ml / 3 fl. oz / ⅓ cup fat-free milk
- a small bunch of flat-leaf parsley
- salt and freshly ground black pepper

Method

1. Add a tablespoon of cubed butter to a large sauté pan set over a moderate heat until hot.

2. Add the mushrooms and a little seasoning, and sauté for 5–6 minutes, stirring and tossing occasionally, until tender.

3. Meanwhile, whisk together the eggs with the milk and the remaining butter. Pour into a heavy-based saucepan set over a medium heat.

4. Cook, stirring frequently, until the egg starts to scramble and thicken.

5. Adjust the seasoning to taste and finely chop some of the parsley.

6. Stir the chopped parsley through the eggs, then spoon it onto plates.

7. Serve with the sautéed mushrooms and the remaining parsley as a garnish.

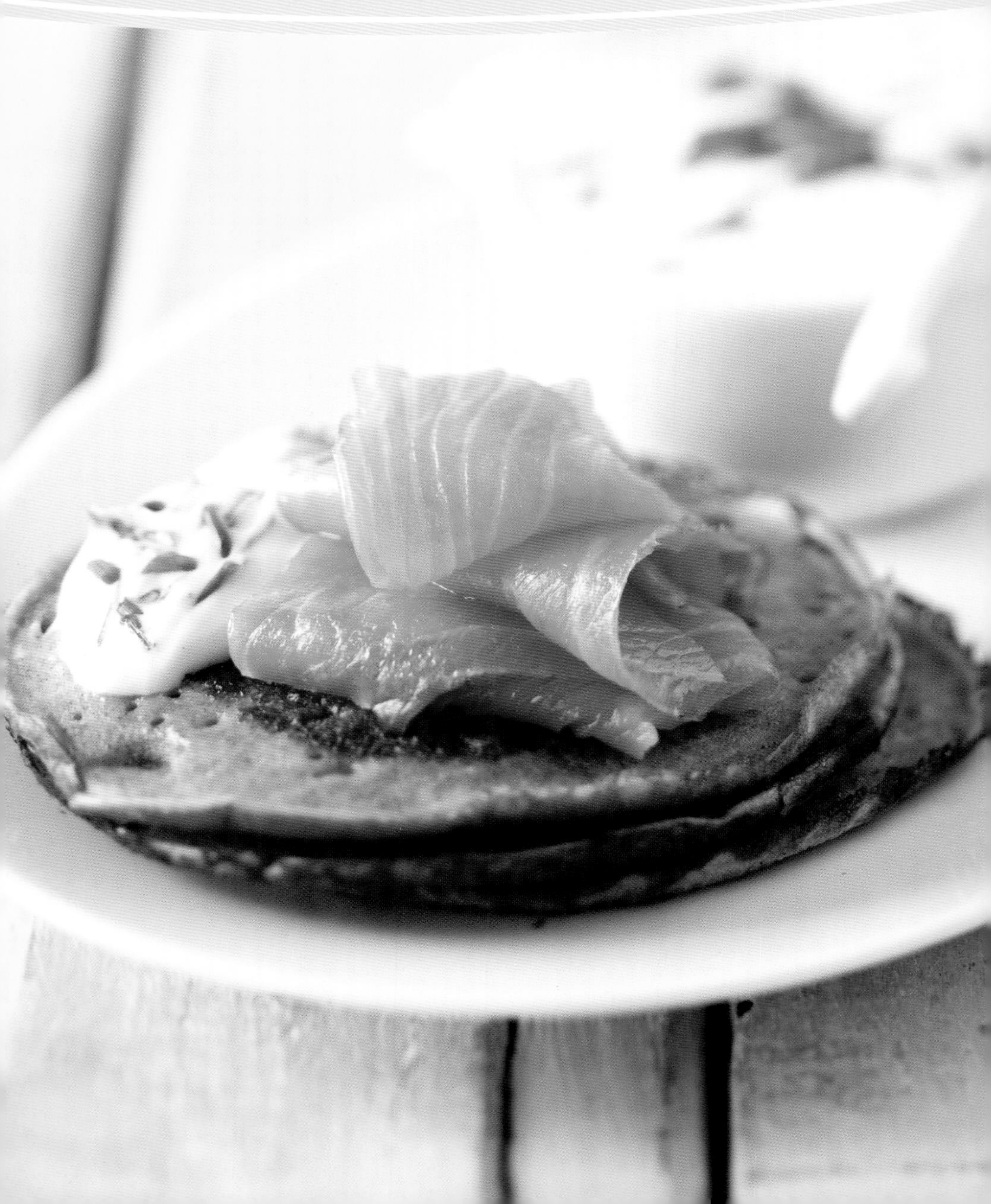

Smoked Salmon Blinis

Serves: **4** | Preparation time: **10 minutes**
Cooking time: **15–20 minutes**

Ingredients

- 50 g / 2 oz / ⅓ cup buckwheat flour
- 110 g / 4 oz / ⅔ cup strong white plain (all-purpose) flour
- ¾ tsp salt
- ½ tsp baking powder
- 1 ½ tsp fast-action dried yeast
- 150 g / 5 oz / ⅔ cup crème fraiche
- 175 ml / 6 fl. oz / ¾ cup semi-skimmed milk
- 2 medium egg yolks
- 2 tbsp unsalted butter
- 150 g / 5 oz / 1 cup smoked salmon slices
- 1 lemon, juiced
- 200 g / 7 oz / 1 cup low-fat yoghurt
- a small bunch of chives, finely chopped

Method

1. Prepare the blini batter by sifting together the flours, salt and baking powder.

2. Sprinkle the yeast on top, then combine the crème fraiche and milk and heat together gently. Remove from the heat and whisk in the egg yolks until smooth. Pour on top of the flour mixture and whisk, then set to one side.

3. Melt the butter in a saucepan, then brush a blini pan with a little melted butter and heat over a moderate heat. Add small ladles of the batter to the pan and cook until set and golden underneath. Flip and cook for 1 minute, then transfer to a lined plate.

4. Stack the blinis on serving plates. Dress the smoked salmon with lemon juice, then sit on top of the stacked blinis.

5. Whisk together the yoghurt and chives and serve on one side.

Light Bites and Lunches

At lunchtime, it's easy to grab a sandwich, or whatever else is available, but it is worth taking the time and effort to eat something healthy.

Soup is a great option for a healthy, sugar-free lunch. Bought soups often have a lot of salt and some added sugar so try making your own. You can make a big batch and freeze it in individual portions.

Salads are another perfect sugar-free choice for lunch. Just make sure you do not undo all your good work by slathering on a sugar-laden dressing. Rather, make your own by mixing olive oil and lemon juice.

The lunch ideas in this section can be eaten at other times of the day, too, and would even work as dinners. Mix and match and see which ones work best for you!

Cherry Tomato Soup

Serves: **4** | Preparation time: **25 minutes**
Cooking time: **50–55 minutes**

Ingredients

- 2 tbsp olive oil
- 1 medium onion, finely chopped
- 1 medium carrot, finely chopped
- 1 stick of celery, finely chopped
- 2 tbsp tomato purée
- 850 g / 1 lb 14 oz / 5 ⅔ cups mixed cherry tomatoes, halved
- 1.2 l / 2 pints / 5 cups vegetable stock
- 175 ml / 6 fl. oz / ¾ cup passata
- a few bay leaves, to garnish
- flaked sea salt and freshly ground black pepper

Method

1. Heat the olive oil in a large saucepan over a medium-low heat until hot, then add the onion, carrot and celery.

2. Sweat for 8–10 minutes with a little salt until they start to brown, then stir in the tomato purée and three-quarters of the cherry tomatoes.

3. Cover the saucepan and allow the tomatoes to stew for 10 minutes over a low heat.

4. Remove the cover after 10 minutes and stir in the stock and passata. Bring to a simmer and cook over a reduced heat for 25–30 minutes, stirring occasionally.

5. Blend the soup with a stick blender until smooth. Return the soup to a simmer in the saucepan and season to taste.

6. Ladle into bowls and garnish with the remaining cherry tomatoes, bay leaves and extra seasoning.

Tuna Stew in Granary Buns

Serves: **4** | Preparation time: **10 minutes**
Cooking time: **15–20 minutes**

Ingredients

- 2 tbsp olive oil
- 2 small courgettes (zucchinis), finely diced
- 2 small carrots, peeled and finely diced
- a small sprig of rosemary, chopped
- 1 clove of garlic, minced
- 300 g / 10 ½ oz / 2 cups canned tuna chunks, drained
- 275 g / 10 oz / 1 ¾ cups passata
- 75 ml / 3 fl. oz / ⅓ cup cold water
- 4 seeded granary buns, split
- salt and freshly ground black pepper

Method

1. Heat the olive oil in a casserole dish set over a medium heat until hot.

2. Add the courgette and carrot with a little seasoning. Sweat for 6–7 minutes, stirring frequently, until softened.

3. Add the rosemary and garlic and cook for 1 minute, then add the tuna, passata and water.

4. Stir well and bring the stew to a gentle simmer. Leave to cook for 8–10 minutes, stirring occasionally, until thickened.

5. Adjust the seasoning to taste and leave the stew to cool slightly before spooning into the granary buns.

6. Serve immediately.

Penne and Seafood Salad

Serves: **4** | Preparation time: **20 minutes**
Cooking time: **12–15 minutes**

Ingredients

- 350 g / 12 oz / 3 cups penne pasta
- 150 g / 5 oz / 3 cups mixed leaf salad
- 2 sheets of dried wakame seaweed
- 2 tbsp sunflower oil
- 300 g / 10 ½ oz piece of salmon fillet, cubed
- 150 g / 5 oz / 1 cup crayfish tails
- a large handful of crispy shredded seaweed
- 75 ml / 3 fl. oz / ⅓ cup dark soy sauce, to serve
- a few sprigs of coriander (cilantro)
- salt and freshly ground black pepper

Method

1. Preheat the grill to hot and cook the pasta in a large saucepan of salted, boiling water until 'al dente'.

2. Drain well and leave to cool to one side. Soak the sheets of wakame seaweed in a bowl of boiling water until tender, then drain and chop.

3. Coat the cubed salmon and crayfish tails in sunflower oil and season well.

4. Arrange on a grilling tray and grill for 4–5 minutes until the salmon is golden and crisp.

5. Remove from the grill and leave to cool for 5 minutes, then toss with the penne pasta, crispy seaweed and wakame seaweed.

6. Season to taste and serve in bowls with the mixed leaf salad, coriander and pots of soy sauce on the side.

Turkey, Brie and Avocado Slices

Serves: **4** | Preparation time: **5 minutes**

Cooking time: **5 minutes**

Ingredients

- 100 g / 3 ½ oz piece of Brie
- 150 g / 5 oz / 1 cup turkey slices
- 4 thick slices of wholemeal baguette
- 1 large ripe avocado, pitted and sliced

Method

1. Cut the piece of Brie into four even slices using a warm, wet knife.

2. Fold the slices of turkey and arrange on top of the slices of baguette.

3. Top with the Brie and then avocado slices; serve immediately.

Lentil Veggie Burger

Serves: **4** | Preparation time: **1 hour 5–15 minutes**
Cooking time: **6–8 minutes**

Ingredients

- 3 tbsp sunflower oil
- 1 small red onion, finely chopped
- 2 cloves of garlic, minced
- 150 g / 5 oz / 1 cup yellow split peas
- 100 g / 3 ½ oz / ½ cup brown rice
- 600 ml / 1 pint 2 fl. oz / 2 ½ cups vegetable stock
- 150 g / 5 oz / 1 cup dried breadcrumbs
- a small bunch of flat-leaf parsley, finely chopped
- 3 tbsp plain yoghurt
- 1 tbsp low-fat mayonnaise
- a pinch of smoked paprika
- 4 seeded burger buns, split
- 1 small Romaine lettuce, leaves separated
- salt and freshly ground black pepper

Method

1. Heat 1 tbsp of sunflower oil over a medium heat. Add the onion and garlic and sweat for 3–4 minutes, then stir in the peas and rice.

2. Stir well and cover with the stock. Bring to a simmer and cook over a low heat, covered, for 50–60 minutes until the peas and rice are tender.

3. Leave the mixture to cool slightly, then spoon into a food processor. Pulse until just combined and tip into a mixing bowl. Add 100 g of the breadcrumbs and the parsley. Mix thoroughly and season. Cover and chill for 30 minutes.

4. Shape the mixture into four thick patties, then coat in the remaining breadcrumbs. Preheat the grill to hot. Drizzle the patties with the remaining oil and grill for 3–4 minutes on both sides.

5. Whisk together the yoghurt, mayonnaise, paprika and a little seasoning. Assemble the buns with lettuces, patties and some sauce, and serve with the bun lids.

Lettuce and Carrot Soup

Serves: **4** | Preparation time: **10 minutes**
Cooking time: **17–20 minutes**

Ingredients

- 2 tbsp olive oil
- 2 sticks of celery, peeled and sliced
- 2 small carrots, peeled and shredded
- 150 g / 5 oz / 2 cups button mushrooms, sliced
- 1 l / 1 pint 16 fl. oz / 4 cups light vegetable stock
- 2 small gem lettuce, sliced
- a small bunch of chives, roughly chopped
- salt and pepper freshly ground black pepper

Method

1. Heat the olive oil in a large saucepan set over a medium heat until hot.
2. Add the celery and a little seasoning, then sweat for 4–5 minutes, stirring occasionally.
3. Add the carrots, mushrooms and stock. Stir well and bring to a simmer, then cook over a reduced heat for 10 minutes.
4. Stir in the lettuce and continue to cook for 3–4 minutes until wilted.
5. Add the chives and adjust the seasoning to taste before ladling into bowls and serving.

Bean and Chicken Salad

Serves: **4** | Preparation time: **10 minutes**
Cooking time: **8–10 minutes**

Ingredients

- 2 tbsp sunflower oil
- 1 tsp dried oregano
- 1 tsp dried basil
- 4 small skinless chicken breasts, trimmed and cut into large strips
- 200 g / 7 oz / 1 cup canned white haricot beans, drained
- 200 g / 7 oz / 1 cup canned butter (lima) beans, drained
- 1 tbsp olive oil
- 1 tbsp lemon juice
- 100 g / 3 ½ oz / 2 cups baby spinach, washed
- 1 red onion, finely sliced
- 1 red chilli (chili), sliced
- 75 g / 3 oz / ½ cup mixed olives
- salt and freshly ground black pepper

Method

1. Preheat the grill to hot.
2. Whisk together the sunflower oil with the dried herbs, then add the chicken strips and toss well to coat.
3. Season the chicken and grill for 8–10 minutes, turning once, until cooked through.
4. Remove from the grill and leave to cool to one side.
5. Toss the beans with the olive oil and lemon juice in a large mixing bowl.
6. Arrange the spinach leaves on serving plates, then top with the chicken, beans, red onion, chilli and olives.
7. Serve immediately.

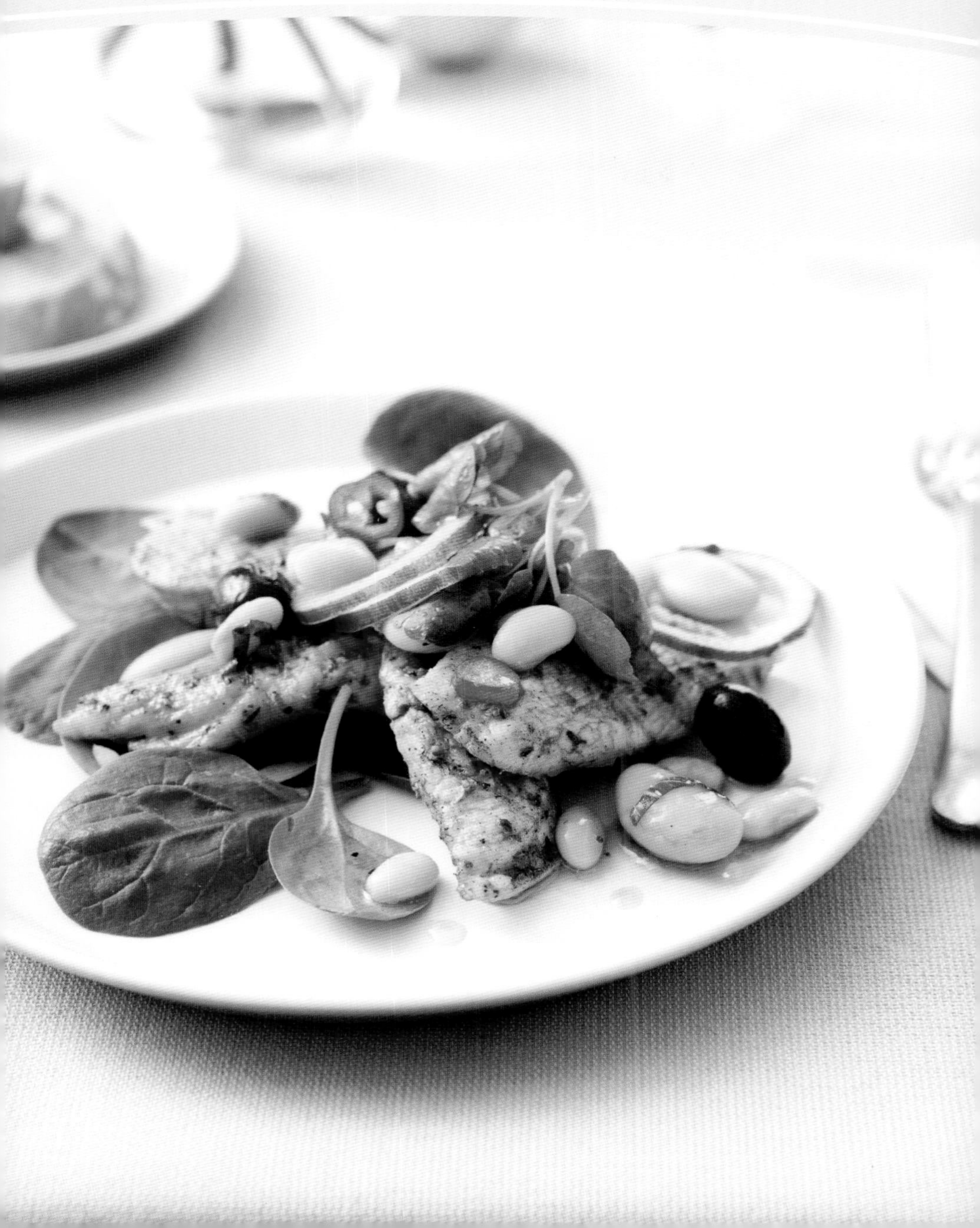

Warm Duck and Veggie Salad

Serves: **4** | Preparation time: **25 minutes**
Cooking time: **15–20 minutes**

Ingredients

- 4 small duck breasts (skin on)
- 2 small red peppers, sliced
- 2 small yellow peppers, sliced
- 1 small head of broccoli, prepared into small florets
- a small bunch of tarragon, chopped
- 3 tbsp plain yoghurt
- 1 tbsp walnuts, crushed
- salt and freshly ground black pepper

Method

1. Lightly score the fat and skin of the ducks breasts. Season well and place skin-side down in a large, heavy-based saucepan.

2. Place the saucepan over a medium heat and let the fat from the duck breasts render down until the skin start to turn golden.

3. Once most of the fat has rendered away, tip most of it away and flip the breasts. Cook for a further 6–8 minutes until the breasts are firm, then remove and drain. Cover loosely with foil and leave to rest for 10 minutes.

4. Add the peppers and broccoli to the pan and cook them in the remaining duck fat, over a medium heat and covered, for 3–4 minutes.

5. Slice the breasts and add them to the pan, then cook for 2–3 minutes. Add the yoghurt and tarragon. Stir well and cook for 1 minute, then season. Serve with crushed walnuts.

Mushroom and Yoghurt

Serves: **4** | Preparation time: **10 minutes**
Cooking time: **5 minutes**

Ingredients

- 300 g / 10 ½ oz / 4 cups button mushrooms
- 200 g / 7 oz / 1 cup low-fat plain yoghurt
- 2 tbsp reduced-fat crème fraiche
- 1 tbsp lemon juice
- a small bunch of chives, finely chopped
- salt and freshly ground black pepper

Method

1. Wash and dry the mushrooms thoroughly, then slice.

2. Whisk together the yoghurt, crème fraiche, lemon juice and seasoning in a small mixing bowl until smooth.

3. Arrange the sliced mushrooms in serving cups and spoon over the yoghurt sauce.

4. Garnish with chopped chives and a little more black pepper before serving.

Lettuce and Turkey Salad

Serves: **4** | Preparation time: **15–20 minutes**
Cooking time: **15 minutes**

Ingredients

- 75 g / 3 oz / ⅓ cup low-fat plain yoghurt
- 1 tbsp low-fat mayonnaise
- 1 tbsp lemon juice
- 1 tsp Worcestershire sauce
- ½ tsp paprika
- 4 small eggs
- 2 x 150 g / 5 oz turkey breast escalopes
- 1 tbsp sunflower oil
- 1 large round lettuce, leaves separated
- 2 spring onions (scallions), finely sliced
- 1 green chilli (chili), finely sliced
- 1 red chilli (chili), finely sliced
- salt and freshly ground black pepper

Method

1. Whisk together the yoghurt, mayonnaise, lemon juice, Worcestershire sauce, paprika and seasoning until smooth. Cover and chill.

2. Cook the eggs in a saucepan of boiling water for 12 minutes, then drain and refresh immediately in iced water.

3. Heat the sunflower oil in a large sauté set over a moderate heat until hot.

4. Season the escalopes, then pan-fry for 3–4 minutes on both sides until golden-brown.

5. Remove from the pan and leave to rest for 1 minute, then slice into thin strips.

6. Roughly tear the lettuce and arrange in serving bowls. Peel and quarter the eggs, then arrange on top of the lettuce with the turkey, spring onion and chillies. Drizzle the prepared dressing over the salads and serve.

Tapenade on Toast

Serves: **8 as an appetiser**
Preparation time: **10 minutes**

Ingredients

- 150 g / 5 oz / 1 cup sun-dried tomatoes in oil
- 55 g / 2 oz / ⅓ cup pitted black olives
- 2 cloves of garlic, chopped
- 2 tbsp preserved anchovy fillets, drained
- 2 tbsp passata
- a small handful of basil leaves, finely chopped
- 1 tbsp lemon juice
- 1 white baguette, cut into thin slices
- salt and freshly ground black pepper

Method

1. Combine the sun-dried tomatoes, black olives, garlic, anchovy fillets, passata and a little seasoning in a food processor.

2. Blitz until a thick tapenade comes together.

3. Scrape into a mixing bowl and stir through the chopped basil and lemon juice. Season to taste.

4. Toast the slices of bread under a hot grill until golden brown on both sides.

5. Remove from the grill and leave to cool, then top with the tapenade and serve.

Pea, Watercress and Carrot Salad

Serves: **4** | Preparation time: **10 minutes**

Cooking time: **1 minutes**

Ingredients

- 1 mango, stoned and flesh chopped
- 75 ml / 3 fl. oz / ⅓ cup sunflower oil
- 2 tbsp white wine vinegar
- 150 g / 5 oz / 1 ½ cups frozen petit pois, thawed
- 2 large carrots, peeled
- 100 g / 3 ½ oz / 2 cups watercress
- a few sprigs of mint, leaves picked
- salt and freshly ground black pepper

Method

1. Blitz together the mango flesh, sunflower oil, white wine vinegar and seasoning in a food processor until smooth. Pour into a jug and chill until needed.

2. Blanch the petit pois in a saucepan of salted, boiling water for 1 minute, then drain and refresh in iced water.

3. Peel ribbons of carrot using a vegetable peeler, then toss with the watercress, petit pois and mint leaves in a large mixing bowl.

4. Divide between serving plates and drizzle with the mango vinaigrette before serving.

Thai Prawn Salad

Serves: **4** | Preparation time: **10 minutes**
Cooking time: **2–3 minutes**

Ingredients

- 1 large clove of garlic, minced
- 2 tbsp fish sauce
- 2 tbsp rice wine vinegar
- 1 lime, juiced
- 2 tbsp light soy sauce
- 2 tbsp sunflower oil
- 350 g / 12 oz / 2 ⅓ cups peeled prawns (shrimp), deveined
- 1 red chilli (chili), finely sliced
- 1 round lettuce, shredded
- ½ small cucumber, julienned
- ½ small onion, finely sliced

Method

1. Whisk together the garlic, fish sauce, vinegar, lime juice and soy sauce in a small bowl, then set to one side.

2. Heat the sunflower oil in a large sauté pan or wok set over a moderate heat until hot.

3. Add the prawns and chilli. Stir-fry for 2–3 minutes until the prawns are pink and tender.

4. Remove from the heat and add two tablespoons of the dressing.

5. Toss the lettuce, cucumber and onion with the remaining dressing and arrange in bowls.

6. Top with the prawns and serve immediately.

Tomato and Pepper Salad

Serves: **4** | Preparation time: **5 minutes**

Cooking time: **5 minutes**

Ingredients

- 2 medium yellow peppers, diced
- 2 medium green peppers, diced
- 4 large vine tomatoes, cored and sliced into wedges
- 2 spring onions (scallions), roughly chopped
- a small bunch of mint leaves
- 55 ml / 2 fl. oz / ¼ cup olive oil
- 1 tbsp white wine vinegar
- 1 tsp Dijon mustard
- 4 small white tortillas, to serve
- 1 tbsp Parmesan, finely grated
- flaked sea salt and freshly ground black pepper

Method

1. Toss together the peppers, tomato wedges and spring onions with a little seasoning in a large mixing bowl.

2. Pick the mint leaves from their stems and roughly chop, then add to mixing bowl.

3. Whisk together the olive oil, vinegar, Dijon mustard and seasoning in a small mixing bowl until smooth.

4. Toss the dressing with the salad to coat evenly.

5. Serve with the tortillas and a sprinkling of Parmesan and flaked sea salt.

Main Meals

You've stuck to your sugar-free diet for breakfast and lunch, and now it is time for a delicious dinner – you deserve it! The recipes in this section will give you loads of ideas for nutritious, sugar-free meals.

Fish is a fantastic choice: it is sugar-free, high in protein and other nutrients, and many types are low-calorie. It can be cooked in many different ways, and is usually quick to prepare, making it perfect for busy days.

Meat fits into a sugar-free diet, too. Stick to lean cuts and remove all visible fat and skin. Like other high-protein foods, meat can help you feel fuller for longer, and it also supplies vital minerals, such as iron.

Any meat or fish on your plate should be accompanied by fresh vegetables. You will quickly get tired of steamed broccoli at every meal, so now is a great time to experiment with vegetables you have never tried before. You may find something new that you absolutely love!

Swordfish with Spring Onions

Serves: **4** | Preparation time: **5 minutes**
Cooking time: **6–8 minutes**

Ingredients

- 4 x 175 g / 6 oz swordfish fillets
- 2 tbsp sunflower oil
- a few sprigs of dill, to garnish
- 100 g / 3 ½ oz / ⅔ cup pitted black olives, chopped
- 4 spring onions (scallions), finely sliced
- salt and freshly ground black pepper

Method

1. Preheat the grill to hot.

2. Brush the swordfish with oil and season generously on both sides.

3. Arrange on a grilling tray and grill for 6–8 minutes, turning once, until the flesh is firm yet slightly springy to the touch.

4. Finely chop some of the dill and sprinkle on top of the swordfish.

5. Transfer to plates and top with chopped olives and sliced spring onion. Garnish with more dill before serving.

Summer Veggie Stir-fry

Serves: **4** | Preparation time: **5 minutes**

Cooking time: **7 minutes**

Ingredients

- 2 tbsp sunflower oil
- 2 medium yellow courgettes (zucchinis), roughly chopped
- 150 g / 5 oz / 1 ½ cups green (string) beans, trimmed
- 150 g / 5 oz / 1 ½ cups asparagus spears, trimmed with woody ends removed
- 4 thin spring onions (scallions)
- 150 g / 5 oz / 1 cup broad (fava) beans, shelled
- 150 g / 5 oz / 1 cup cherry tomatoes, halved
- a small bunch of basil, leaves picked
- salt and freshly ground black pepper

Method

1. Blanch the courgette in a saucepan of salted, boiling water for 2 minutes. Remove with a slotted spoon, then add the green beans and asparagus spears.

2. Blanch for 1 minute, then drain and pat dry. Heat a tablespoon of oil in a large wok set over a moderate heat until hot.

3. Add the courgette and stir-fry for 2 minutes, then add the beans, asparagus spears and spring onions.

4. Stir-fry for a further minute with a little seasoning, then add the remaining oil as well as the broad beans and cherry tomato halves.

5. Continue to stir-fry for another minute and adjust the seasoning to taste. Serve in a large bowl, garnished with basil leaves on top.

Stuffed Round Courgettes

Serves: **4** | Preparation time: **15 minutes**
Cooking time: **30–35 minutes**

Ingredients

- 4 medium round courgettes (zucchinis)
- 100 g / 3 ½ oz / 1 ⅓ cups fresh breadcrumbs
- 75 g / 3 oz / ¾ cup mozzarella, grated
- 50 g / 2 oz / ⅓ cup sun-dried tomatoes, chopped
- 2 tbsp olive oil
- salt and freshly ground black pepper

Method

1. Preheat the oven to 180°C (160°C fan) / 350F / gas 4.
2. Score light patterns in the skin of the courgettes using the edge of a peeler, then remove the tops and reserve.
3. Scoop out most of the flesh and seeds, discarding them.
4. Mix together the breadcrumbs, mozzarella, sun-dried tomatoes and seasoning, then spoon into the cavities.
5. Replace the tops on top of the stuffing and arrange the courgettes on a baking tray.
6. Drizzle with olive oil and bake for 30–35 minutes until the flesh is tender and the filling is piping hot.
7. Remove from the oven and leave to cool slightly before serving.

Veggie Sausage Pasta

Serves: **4** | Preparation time: **15–20 minutes**
Cooking time: **15–20 minutes**

Ingredients

- 350 g / 12 oz / 3 cups penne pasta
- 1 ½ tbsp sunflower oil
- 1 medium onion, finely chopped
- 1 clove of garlic, minced
- 75 g / 3 oz / 1 cup button mushrooms, finely chopped
- 400 g / 14 oz / 2 cups canned chopped tomatoes
- 4 vegetarian/soy sausages
- a few sprigs of oregano, chopped
- salt and freshly ground black pepper

Method

1. Cook the pasta in a large saucepan of salted, boiling water until 'al dente'.

2. Meanwhile, heat the oil in a large saucepan set over a moderate heat until hot. Sauté the onion and garlic with a pinch of salt for 5–6 minutes, stirring frequently, until softened.

3. Add the mushrooms and continue to cook for 3–4 minutes, then add the chopped tomatoes.

4. Stir well and bring the sauce to a simmer, then reduce to a low heat and cook for 8–10 minutes until thickened.

5. Drain the pasta well and cover loosely.

6. Heat the grill to hot and grill the sausages for 6–7 minutes, turning occasionally. Remove from the grill, slice, and stir in to the sauce.

7. Adjust the seasoning to taste, then stir into the pasta and serve with chopped oregano on top.

Halibut with Concasse

Serves: **4** | Preparation time: **10 minutes**
Cooking time: **10–12 minutes**

Ingredients

- 450 g / 1 lb piece of halibut, skinned and pin-boned
- 350 g / 12 oz / 2 ½ cups vine tomatoes, cored and finely chopped
- 75 g / 3 oz / ½ cup pitted black olives, chopped
- 2 tbsp sunflower oil
- a small bunch of basil, leaves picked
- salt and freshly ground black pepper

Method

1. Preheat the oven to 200°C (180°C fan) / 400F / gas 6.

2. Use a sharp knife to cut the halibut into four, even fillets.

3. Sit the fillets in a cast-iron or heavy-based sauté pan, then season generously.

4. Roughly mash the chopped tomatoes in a mixing bowl, then spoon on top of the fillets and top with the olives.

5. Drizzle the oil over everything and roast in the oven for 10–12 minutes; the fish will be firm yet very slightly springy to the touch when it is ready.

6. Remove the pan from the oven and garnish with the basil leaves before serving.

Salmon Satay Brochettes

Serves: **4** | Preparation time: **15 minutes**
Cooking time: **6–8 minutes**

Ingredients

- 150 g / 5 oz / 1 ½ cups roasted peanuts
- ½ tsp salt
- 1 tbsp groundnut oil
- 55 ml / 2 fl. oz / ¼ cup warm water
- 1 tbsp light soy sauce
- 1 tbsp lime juice
- 450 g / 14 oz / 3 cups skinless salmon fillet, diced
- 350 g / 12 oz / 2 cups cooked long-grain rice
- 8 wooden skewers, soaked in cold water for 30 minutes beforehand
- 2 spring onions (scallions), finely sliced

Method

1. Blitz together the peanuts and salt in a food processor for 30–45 seconds. Scrape down the sides and continue to blitz, adding the oil slowly, until you have a smooth peanut butter.

2. Whisk together the peanut butter, water, soy sauce and lime juice in a saucepan until smooth.

3. Cook over a medium-low heat for 2–3 minutes, stirring, until simmering. Remove from the heat and cool for 5 minutes. Preheat the grill to hot.

4. Thread the salmon onto the skewers and brush with a little of the satay sauce.

5. Arrange the salmon skewers on a grilling tray. Grill for 4–5 minutes, turning once, until the flesh is firm yet slightly springy to the touch.

6. Reheat the rice, then spoon into bowls.

7. Sit the brochettes on top, brush with satay sauce and serve garnished with spring onion.

Asian-style Pork Burger

Serves: **4** | Preparation time: **30–35 minutes**
Cooking time: **8–10 minutes**

Ingredients

- 175 g / 6 oz / 2 cups red jalapeno or chilli (chili) peppers, deseeded and chopped
- 2 cloves of garlic, minced
- 75 ml / 3 fl. oz / ⅓ cup distilled white vinegar
- 2 tbsp tomato paste
- 1 tbsp fish sauce
- 150 g / 3 oz / ⅔ cup low-fat yoghurt
- ½ tsp garlic powder
- a small bunch of dill, finely chopped
- 4 crusty white rolls, split
- 4 x 175 g / 6 oz pork loin steaks
- 1 tbsp sunflower oil
- 1 lime, juiced
- 1 tbsp fish sauce
- ½ white cabbage, shredded
- a few large sprigs of coriander (cilantro), to garnish
- salt and freshly ground black pepper

Method

1. Combine the chillies, garlic, vinegar, tomato paste, fish sauce and 1 tsp of salt in a food processor, and blitz until smooth. Pour into a pan and bring to the boil over a moderate heat. Reduce the heat and simmer for 5–10 minutes. Season and set to one side.

2. Whisk together the yoghurt, garlic powder and dill with seasoning. Cover and chill. Flatten the steaks and slice each in half.

3. Whisk together the chilli sauce, oil, lime juice and fish sauce with a little pepper. Add the pork pieces and rub the marinade into them, then cover and leave for 15 minutes.

4. Preheat a grill until hot. Remove the pork shake off any excess marinade. Cook under the grill for 8–10 minutes, turning once.

5. Spread yoghurt sauce onto the bun bases, top with cabbage and pieces of pork, and serve garnished with coriander and the bun lids.

Grilled Salmon with Lettuce

Serves: **4** | Preparation time: **10 minutes**
Cooking time: **8–10 minutes**

Ingredients

- 75 g / 3 oz / ⅓ cup low-fat yoghurt
- 2 tbsp cold water
- 2 tbsp white wine vinegar
- 1 tbsp Dijon mustard
- 1 tbsp olive oil
- 4 x 150 g / 5 oz pieces of salmon
- 2 tbsp harissa paste
- 2 little gem lettuces, quartered
- 2 large cloves of garlic, thinly sliced
- ½ red onion, finely sliced
- 1 lemon, zest pared and thinly sliced
- 2 tbsp sunflower oil
- salt and freshly ground black pepper

Method

1. Preheat the grill to a moderately hot temperature. Whisk together the yoghurt, water, vinegar, mustard and olive oil with a little seasoning until smooth and pour into a jug, chilling until needed.

2. Rub the tops of the salmon with harissa and arrange on a large grilling tray.

3. Sit the quartered lettuce next to the salmon and top with garlic, onion and lemon zest.

4. Drizzle the lettuce and salmon with sunflower oil and seasoning and grill for 6–8 minutes. Remove the lettuce after 5 minutes (the salmon will need a few extra minutes).

5. Once the salmon is firm with a spring to the touch, remove from the grill and place on plates next to the lettuce halves. Spoon a little of the prepared dressing around the plate and serve.

Asparagus and Prosciutto Salad

Serves: **4** | Preparation time: **5–10 minutes**
Cooking time: **10–13 minutes**

Ingredients

- 4 medium eggs
- 8 thick spears of white asparagus, woody ends removed
- 150 g / 5 oz / 1 cup prosciutto slices
- 55 g / 2 oz / 1 cup watercress, washed and dried
- 400 g / 14 oz / 2 cups canned artichoke hearts, drained and roughly chopped
- 2 tbsp olive oil
- salt and freshly ground black pepper

Method

1. Cook the eggs in a large saucepan of boiling water for 8–10 minutes. Drain and refresh immediately in iced water.

2. Peel the asparagus spears to remove the outer layer, then blanch in a saucepan of salted, boiling water for 2–3 minutes.

3. Drain well and leave to cool.

4. Roughly tear the slices of prosciutto and arrange on plates along with the watercress and artichoke.

5. Carefully crack and peel the eggs, then cut in half and sit next to the salad.

6. Drizzle the salad with olive oil and finish with a little salt and freshly ground black pepper before serving.

Chicken with Vegetables

Serves: **6** | Preparation time: **25 minutes**
Cooking time: **1 hour 30–40 minutes**

Ingredients

- 1.5 kg / 3 lb 5 oz chicken, cleaned and trussed
- 2 tbsp sunflower oil
- 5 small carrots
- 3 medium purple carrots
- 3 medium parsnips
- 2 small lemons, halved
- a small bunch of flat-leaf parsley, chopped
- salt and freshly ground black pepper

Method

1. Preheat the oven to 180°C (160°C fan) / 350F / gas 4 and rub the chicken with a tablespoon of oil. Season generously.

2. Arrange the carrots and parsnips in the base of a roasting tin and drizzle with the remaining oil.

3. Season generously, then tuck the lemon halves between the vegetables.

4. Sit the chicken on top and place the roasting tin in the oven for 1 hour 30–40 minutes until the chicken is cooked through; the juices should run clear when the thickest part of the thigh is pierced.

5. Remove from the oven and cover loosely with aluminium foil. Leave to rest for at least 15 minutes.

6. Sprinkle the vegetables with chopped parsley before serving.

Marinated Vegetable Pizza

Serves: **4** | Preparation time: **40 minutes**
Cooking time: **12–15 minutes**

Ingredients

- 1 medium aubergine (eggplant), deseeded and cut into thin strips
- 1 large red pepper, sliced
- 1 medium onion, roughly sliced
- 2 tbsp olive oil
- 150 g / 5 oz ready-made pizza dough
- 55 g / 2 oz / ½ cup Manchego, grated
- 55 g / 2 oz / ½ cup mozzarella, grated
- 2 tbsp preserved anchovy fillets, drained and roughly chopped
- a small bunch of chives, finely chopped
- a little plain (all-purpose) flour, for dusting

Method

1. Combine the aubergine, peppers and onion in a mixing bowl with the oil and a little seasoning. Stir well and leave at room temperature for up to 30 minutes.

2. Preheat the oven to 220°C (200°C fan) / 425F / gas 7 and line a large, square baking tray. Roll out the dough on a floured surface into a square approximately 25 cm x 25 cm x ½ cm (10 in x 10 in x ¼ in).

3. Carefully lift onto the prepared baking tray and top with the grated cheeses and anchovy, then top with the marinated vegetables and oil.

4. Bake for 12–15 minutes until the dough is cooked and golden brown at the edges. Remove to a wire rack to briefly cool, then sprinkle with chopped chives and serve.

Turkey Burger

Serves: **4** | Preparation time: **15 minutes**
Cooking time: **18–22 minutes**

Ingredients

- 100 g / 3 ½ oz / ½ cup tomato purée
- 1 tbsp apple cider vinegar
- a pinch of allspice
- a pinch of Cayenne pepper
- ½ tsp garlic powder
- ½ tsp onion powder
- 75 ml / 3 fl. oz / ⅓ cup cold water
- 4 sesame seed burger buns, split
- 450 g / 1 lb / 3 cups lean turkey mince
- 75 g / 3 ½ oz / 1 cup fresh white breadcrumbs
- 1 tbsp sunflower oil
- 2 large vine tomatoes, cored and chopped
- ½ red onion, finely chopped
- 1 small shallot, finely chopped
- a small bunch of basil, roughly chopped
- salt and freshly ground black pepper

Method

1. Preheat the oven to 190°C (170°C fan) / 375F / gas 5. Whisk together the tomato purée, vinegar, allspice, Cayenne, garlic powder, onion powder and water. Season to taste, then cover and chill.

2. Scrunch together the turkey mince and breadcrumbs with seasoning in a mixing bowl. Divide the mixture into four, the pack down and shape into patties. Arrange on a baking tray and drizzle with the oil.

3. Bake for 18–22 minutes until golden on the outside and cooked through on the inside.

4. Meanwhile, stir together the tomato, red onion, shallot and basil with a little seasoning in a mixing bowl. Cover and chill until ready to serve.

5. Spread the bun bases with the prepared ketchup, then sit the patties on top and spoon over some salsa. Serve with the bun lids.

Grilled Salmon with Vegetables

Serves: **4** | Preparation time: **15 minutes**
Cooking time: **18–22 minutes**

Ingredients

- 1 tbsp olive oil
- 250 g / 9 oz / 1 ⅔ cups baby turnips, trimmed
- 150 g / 5 oz / 1 cup baby carrots, trimmed
- 450 ml / 16 fl. oz / 2 cups vegetable stock
- 150 g / 5 oz / 1 cup asparagus spears, trimmed with woody ends removed
- 4 small gem lettuce, split in half
- 75 g / 3 oz / 1 cup chestnut mushrooms, halved
- 4 x 150 g / 5 oz pieces of salmon
- 2 small cooked beets, halved
- salt and freshly ground black pepper

Method

1. Heat the olive oil in a large saucepan set over a moderate heat until hot. Add the turnips and carrots and sauté with seasoning for 2 minutes

2. Cover with the stock and simmer for 7–8 minutes, then add the asparagus and lettuce.

3. Continue to simmer for 2 minutes, then stir in the mushrooms and remove from the heat. Set to one side.

4. Preheat the grill to hot and season the salmon well before arranging, skin-side up, on a grilling tray. Grill for 7–9 minutes until the skin is crisp and the flesh is turning opaque.

5. To serve, remove the vegetables from the cooking liquor with a pair of tongs and arrange in the centre of plates.

6. Sit the salmon on top and garnish with a halved beet before serving.

Chilli con Carne with Rice

Serves: **4** | Preparation time: **15–20 minutes**
Cooking time: **40–50 minutes**

Ingredients

- 1 ½ tbsp sunflower oil
- 1 large onion, finely chopped
- 2 cloves of garlic, minced
- 2 tsp ground cumin
- 1 tsp ground coriander (cilantro)
- 1 tsp chilli (chili) powder
- ½ tsp dried oregano
- 450 g / 1 lb / 3 cups extra lean steak mince
- 400 g / 14 oz / 2 cups canned chopped tomatoes
- 200 g / 7 oz / 1 cup canned kidney beans, drained
- 350 g / 12 oz / 2 cups cooked basmati rice
- 55 g / 2 oz / ¼ cup low-fat plain yoghurt
- salt and freshly ground black pepper

Method

1. Heat the oil in a large, heavy-based saucepan set over a medium heat until hot. Add the onion and garlic and sweat for 6–7 minutes, stirring occasionally.

2. Add the ground spices and herbs and stir well. Cook for 30 seconds, then add the mince. Increase the heat and cook until browned, breaking it up with a wooden spoon.

3. Stir in the chopped tomatoes and kidney beans until incorporated, then cover with a lid and simmer over a reduced heat for 30–40 minutes; stir to prevent sticking.

4. Season to taste and leave to cool for a few minutes as you reheat the rice in a microwave until piping hot.

5. Spoon the rice into bowls and top with the chilli. Garnish with a dollop of yoghurt and a little seasoning on top before serving.

Squid and Veggie Wok-fry

Serves: **4** | Preparation time: **5 minutes**
Cooking time: **5 minutes**

Ingredients

- 2 tbsp groundnut oil
- 350 g / 12 oz / 2 ⅓ cups squid tentacles, cut into rings
- 1 small head of broccoli, prepared into small florets
- 2 medium carrots, peeled and cut into thin batons
- 1 small green pepper, roughly sliced
- 1 small red pepper, roughly sliced
- 110 g / 4 oz / 1 ½ cups beansprouts
- ½ tsp dried chilli (chili) flakes
- 1 tbsp white sesame seeds
- 2 tbsp dark soy sauce
- 1 tbsp rice wine vinegar

Method

1. Heat a tablespoon of oil in a large wok set over a high heat until hot.

2. Add the squid rings and stir-fry for 1 minute, then remove from the wok to a plate.

3. Add the remaining tablespoon of oil, then add the broccoli and carrots. Stir-fry for 2 minutes, then add the peppers and beansprouts.

4. Return the squid rings to the wok and continue to stir-fry for 1–2 minutes. Stir in the chilli flakes, sesame seeds, soy sauce and rice wine vinegar.

5. Spoon into bowls and serve immediately.

Beef and Veggie Stir-fry

Serves: **4** | Preparation time: **5–10 minutes**
Cooking time: **7 minutes**

Ingredients

- 2 tbsp groundnut oil
- 450 g / 1 lb skirt steak, trimmed and sliced
- 1 large head of broccoli, prepared into bite-sized florets
- 2 small red peppers, finely sliced
- 2 spring onions (scallions), sliced diagonally
- 2 tbsp light soy sauce
- 1 tbsp rice wine vinegar
- 1 tbsp white sesame seeds
- 1 orange, zest julienned
- 350 g / 12 oz / 2 cups cooked short-grain rice
- salt and freshly ground black pepper

Method

1. Heat a tablespoon of the groundnut oil in a large wok set over a high temperature until hot.

2. Season the steak with salt and pepper, then stir-fry in the oil for 2 minutes. Remove from the wok.

3. Add the remaining tablespoon of oil and stir-fry the broccoli for 2 minutes, then add the peppers and spring onions and cook for a further minute.

4. Return the steak to the pan and cook over a reduced heat for a further 2 minutes. Season to taste with soy sauce and rice wine vinegar.

5. Stir through the sesame seeds and julienned orange zest at this point.

6. Reheat the rice, if necessary, and serve alongside the stir-fry.

Desserts

Going sugar free doesn't have to mean giving up dessert. If you are reducing rather than eliminating your sugar intake, then dessert can be the time to reward yourself with a small, sweet treat. Even if you are cutting out sugar entirely, there's still room for the occasional pudding. You'll probably find that as your body gets used to a sugar-free diet, you stop craving sweet treats after meals.

Why not choose a coffee? It makes a great way to finish off a meal. If you want something sweet, fresh fruit is a good option.

You'll probably be surprised at the number of sweet desserts that can be made without sugar. Some use sugar substitutes but others use the natural sweetness of ingredients such as fruit. Do a bit of experimenting and you will find something you love.

Lemon Yoghurt Ice Cream

Makes: **1 pint** | Preparation time: **3 hours 25–30 minutes**

Ingredients

- 500 g / 1 lb 2 oz / 2 cups low-fat lemon yoghurt
- 75 ml / 3 fl. oz / ⅓ cup semi-skimmed milk
- 2 tsp lemon extract
- 1 lemon, zested

Method

1. Combine the yoghurt, milk and lemon extract in a food processor. Blitz until smooth.

2. Pour the liquid into an ice cream machine and churn for 15–20 minutes until frozen and creamy.

3. Scrape the frozen yoghurt into a freezer-proof container and freeze until set.

4. Before serving the frozen yoghurt, remove from the freezer and leave to stand for 5 minutes, the scoop out and serve with lemon zest sprinkled on top.

Summer Fruit Jelly

Serves: **4** | Preparation time: **4 hours 10 minutes**

Ingredients

- 225 g / 8 oz / 1 ½ cups strawberries, hulled and chopped
- 150 g / 5 oz / 1 cup raspberries
- 110 g / 4 oz / ¾ cup blackberries
- 75 g / 3 oz / ¾ cup redcurrants
- 2 tbsp sugar-free raspberry jelly powder
- 250 ml / 9 fl. oz / 1 cup boiling water
- 325 ml / 11 fl. oz / 1 ⅓ cups cold water
- 75 g / 3 oz / 1/3 cup low-fat plain yoghurt

Method

1. Grease and line four individual ramekins with a sheet of cling film; make sure that the cling film overhangs the rims.

2. Fill the ramekins with a selection of the fruits, leaving a little fruit for a garnish.

3. Half fill a mixing jug with boiling water and sprinkle over the jelly powder. Leave to dissolve for a few minutes, whisk, and then mix in the cold water.

4. Divide the liquid between the ramekins and transfer to the fridge to set for at least 4 hours or overnight.

5. Once set, carefully lift the jellies out of the ramekins and peel away the cling film.

6. Garnish with the reserved fruit and a dollop of yoghurt on the side.

Fruit Gazpacho

Serves: **4–6** | Preparation time: **5 minutes**

Ingredients

- 3 large ripe bananas
- 200 g / 7 oz / 1 cup canned pineapple chunks in juice
- 375 ml / 13 fl. oz / 1 ½ cups pineapple juice
- 55 ml / 2 fl. oz / ¼ cup white rum (optional)

Method

1. Roughly chop the bananas and combine with three-quarters of the pineapple chunks (and their juice) as well as the pineapple juice and rum, if using.

2. Blitz until the mixture is creamy and pourable.

3. Pour into a serving jug and serve immediately with the remaining pineapple chunks on top.

Almond Jelly

Makes: **4** | Preparation time: **6 hours 10 minutes**

Cooking time: **10 minutes**

Ingredients

- 4 tsp gelatine powder
- 600 ml / 1 pint 2 fl. oz / 3 cups plain almond milk
- ½ tsp vanilla extract
- ½ tsp almond extract
- 2 tbsp almonds, to garnish

Method

1. Grease the insides of four individual ramekins with non-stick cooking spray. Mix the gelatine with two tablespoons of cold water in a small bowl and leave for 2 minutes.

2. Combine the almond milk and vanilla and almond extract in a saucepan, then bring to a simmer over a medium heat.

3. Remove from the heat and pour a little into the gelatine mixture. Whisk and leave for 1 minute, then whisk back into the almond milk in the saucepan. Let the liquid cool slightly, then divide between the ramekins and cover and chill for at least 6 hours until set.

4. Once set, dip the ramekins into a bowl of boiling water and carefully tip out onto plates.

5. Crush some of the almonds and spoon on top as a garnish, serving the rest on the side.

Fraisier-style Verrine

Serves: **4** | Preparation time: **15 minutes**

Cooking time: **5 minutes**

Ingredients

- 4 tsp gelatine powder
- 600 ml / 1 pint 2 fl. oz / 3 cups plain almond milk
- ½ tsp vanilla extract
- ½ tsp almond extract
- 2 tbsp almonds, to garnish

Method

1. Grease the insides of four individual ramekins with non-stick cooking spray. Mix the gelatine with two tablespoons of cold water in a small bowl and leave for 2 minutes.

2. Combine the almond milk, vanilla and almond extract in a saucepan, then bring to a simmer over a medium heat.

3. Remove from the heat and pour a little into the gelatine mixture. Whisk and leave for 1 minute, then whisk back into the almond milk in the saucepan. Let the liquid cool slightly, then divide between the ramekins and cover and chill for at least 6 hours until set.

4. Once set, dip the ramekins into a bowl of boiling water and carefully tip out onto plates.

5. Crush some of the almonds and spoon on top as a garnish, serving the rest on the side.

Iced Lemon Mousse

Serves: 4 | Preparation time: **2 hours 15 minutes**

Cooking time: **5 minutes**

Ingredients

- 2 tsp powdered gelatine
- 75 ml / 3 fl. oz / ⅓ cup no added sugar lemon squash
- 3 medium egg whites
- ½ tsp cream of tartar
- a pinch of salt
- 1 lemon, zested

Method

1. Soften the gelatine in 2 tbsp of cold water in a bowl. Leave to stand for 5 minutes, then whisk.

2. Combine the squash with 250 ml / 9 fl. oz / 1 cup of cold water in a saucepan. Warm over a medium heat, then whisk in the gelatine mixture.

3. Continue to cook for 2 minutes until the gelatine has dissolved. Set to one side to cool.

4. Meanwhile, beat the egg whites with a pinch of salt until soft peaks form. Add the cream of tartar and 2 tbsp of the lemon cordial liquid and beat until stiffly peaked.

5. Divide the remaining lemon squash liquid between four serving glasses.

6. Top with the egg whites and freeze immediately for at least 2 hours.

7. Remove from the freezer and garnish with lemon zest before serving.

Pumpkin and Almond Cake

Serves: **8** | Preparation time: **10 minutes**
Cooking time: **50–60 minutes**

Ingredients

- 300 g / 10 ½ oz / 2 cups canned pumpkin chunks, drained
- 1 tsp vanilla extract
- ½ tsp ground nutmeg
- 150 g / 5 oz / ⅔ cups pumpkin purée, sweetened with agave or honey
- 3 medium eggs
- 150 ml / 5 fl. oz / ⅔ cup sunflower oil
- 2 tbsp semi-skimmed milk
- 200 g / 7 oz / 1 ⅓ cups self-raising flour
- 55 g / 2 oz / ⅓ cup cornflour (cornstarch)
- ½ tsp baking powder
- a pinch of salt
- 55 g / 2 oz / ½ cup ground almonds
- 2 tbsp flaked (slivered) almonds

Method

1. Preheat the oven to 160°C (140°C fan) / 325F / gas 3. Grease and line a 2 lb loaf tin.

2. Add 200 g of pumpkin, the nutmeg and vanilla extract to a food processor. Blitz until smooth.

3. Whisk together the pumpkin purée, eggs, oil and milk in a mixing jug until smooth.

4. Sift the flour, cornflour, baking powder and salt into a mixing bowl, then stir through the ground almonds and remaining pumpkin.

5. Add the wet ingredients to the dry and mix until just incorporated, then scrape into the prepared tin. Tap the tin a few times to release any trapped air bubbles, and scatter the flaked almonds on top.

6. Bake for 50–60 minutes until golden and risen; a toothpick should come out clean from the centre.

7. Remove to a wire rack to cool completely before turning out and slicing.

Light Raspberry Mousse

Serves: **4** | Preparation time: **2 hours 10 minutes**

Cooking time: **5 minutes**

Ingredients

- 350 g / 12 oz / 2 ⅓ cups raspberries
- ½ lemon, juiced
- 400 g / 14 oz / 2 cups coconut cream, chilled
- a pinch of cocoa powder, to garnish

Method

1. Combine 275 g of the raspberries with the lemon juice in a saucepan.

2. Cook over a medium heat, stirring occasionally, until the raspberries are soft and juicy; 4–5 minutes.

3. Purée the mixture in a food processor. Pass through a sieve into a small bowl and set to one side.

4. Whip the coconut cream in a mixing bowl with an electric mixer for 3–4 minutes until softly peaked.

5. Fold through the raspberry purée until evenly incorporated, then spoon into glasses. Cover and chill for 2 hours.

6. Serve the mousses with the reserved raspberries on top and a pinch of cocoa powder as a garnish.

Fromage Blanc and Bilberry Pie

Serves: **8** | Preparation time: **15–20 minutes**
Cooking time: **20–25 minutes**

Ingredients

- 250 g / 9 oz ready-made lighter shortcrust pastry
- a little plain (all-purpose) flour, for dusting
- 1 small egg, beaten
- 350 g / 12 oz / 1 ½ cups fromage blanc
- 350 g / 12 oz / 1 ½ cups vanilla yoghurt
- 1 tbsp lemon juice
- ½ tsp vanilla extract
- 300 g / 10 ½ oz / 2 cups bilberries (use blueberries if not available)

Method

1. Preheat the oven to 180°C (160°C fan) / 350F / gas 4. Roll out the pastry on a floured surface into a round roughly ½ cm (¼ in) thick. Use to line the base and sides of a 20 cm (8 in) fluted tart tin. Trim any excess pastry and discard, then prick the base all over with a fork.

2. Line with greaseproof paper and fill with baking beans, then blind bake for 15–18 minutes. Remove from the oven and discard the greaseproof paper and baking beans.

3. Return the pastry to the oven for 5 minutes to brown the base. Brush with the beaten egg, then return to the oven for another 2 minutes.

4. Allow to cool. Beat together the fromage blanc, yoghurt, lemon juice and vanilla extract.

5. Remove the pastry from the tin, then fill with the fromage blanc filling. Top with most of the bilberries, serving the rest on the side as a garnish.

Buckwheat Waffles

Serves: **4** | Preparation time: **10 minutes**
Cooking time: **15 minutes**

Ingredients

- 150 g / 5 oz / 1 cup plain (all-purpose) flour
- 150 g / 5 oz / 1 cup buckwheat flour
- 1 tbsp baking powder
- ½ tsp salt
- 2 large eggs, beaten
- 375 ml / 13 fl. oz / 1 ½ cups semi-skimmed milk
- 75 g / 3 oz / ⅓ cup unsalted butter, melted
- ½ tsp vanilla extract
- 1 tbsp sunflower oil
- 300 g / 10 ½ oz / 2 cups strawberries, hulled and halved
- 100 g / 3 ½ oz / ⅔ cup soft goats' cheese, cubed
- a small handful of sorrel leaves
- freshly ground black pepper

Method

1. Sift together the flours, baking powder and salt into a large mixing bowl.

2. Beat together the eggs, milk, melted butter and vanilla extract in a mixing jug. Slowly add to the dry ingredients, whisking at the same time until you have a smooth batter.

3. Preheat a waffle iron to hot and wipe the surface with sunflower oil. Ladle the batter into the iron and close. Cook according to manufacturer's instructions until the waffles are golden. Repeat this method to cook the batter until you have four large waffles.

4. Roughly mash half of the strawberries and set to one side. Stack the waffles in bowls and top with mashed strawberries, halved strawberries and some goats' cheese.

5. Garnish with sorrel leaves and a little black pepper before serving.

Carob Coconut Vegan Cake

Makes: **16 squares** | Preparation time: **15 minutes**
Cooking time: **40–45 minutes**

Ingredients

- 250 g / 9 oz / 1 ⅔ cups carob chips
- 150 g / 5 oz / ¾ cup silken tofu
- 250 ml / 9 fl. oz / 1 cup coconut milk
- 175 ml / 6 fl. oz / ¾ cup sunflower oil
- 110 g / 4 oz / ⅔ cup cocoa powder, sifted
- 400 g / 14 oz / 2 ⅔ cups self-raising flour, sifted
- 1 tsp bicarbonate of (baking) soda
- 2 tbsp desiccated coconut
- 2 tbsp flaked (slivered) almonds, toasted

Method

1. Preheat the oven to 180°C (160°C fan) / 350F / gas 4. Grease and line a 20 cm (8 in) square cake tin with greaseproof paper.

2. Melt the carob chips in a bain-marie set over a pan of simmering water. Stir until melted, then set to one side to cool.

3. Combine the tofu, coconut milk, sunflower oil, cocoa powder, flour and bicarbonate of soda in a food processor. Blitz until smooth, then pour into a mixing bowl.

4. Fold through the melted carob chips until incorporated, then scrape the batter into the cake tin and bake for 40–45 minutes.

5. Remove to a wire rack to cool completely, then turn out and cut into squares. Garnish with desiccated coconut and flaked almonds.

Chocolate and Raspberry Mousse

Serves: **4** | Preparation time: **1 hour 10 minutes**
Cooking time: **5 minutes**

Ingredients

- 350 g / 12 oz / 2 ⅓ cups raspberries
- ½ lemon, juiced
- 400 g / 14 oz / 2 cups coconut cream, chilled
- 2 tbsp cocoa powder
- 1 tsp vanilla extract
- ½ tsp xanthan gum

Method

1. Combine three-quarters of the raspberries with the lemon juice in a saucepan set over a medium heat; cook until softened and juicy.

2. Purée the mixture in a food processor and pass through a sieve into a bowl.

3. Scrape the coconut cream into a bowl and add the cocoa powder, vanilla extract and xanthan gum; beat with an electric mixer for 4–5 minutes until thick and softly peaked.

4. Spoon the raspberry purée into the base of four small serving glasses before topping with the remaining raspberries.

5. Spoon the chocolate mousse on top; cover and chill for 1 hour before serving.

Treats and Snacks

Snacking can be one of the biggest pitfalls for someone going sugar free. If your body is used to the constant highs and lows of a sugar-heavy diet, you will probably crave frequent snacks between meals. Unfortunately, some of the most convenient snacks are loaded with sugar.

As you change your diet to a slow-burning, nutrient-rich plan, you will feel fuller for longer and have fewer cravings. But there's no harm in keeping your energy up throughout the day with a healthy snack here and there.

There are loads of options for healthy snacks. A handful of nuts, for example, is packed with protein, so why not keep some handy in your bag or your desk drawer? Vegetables dipped in hummus make another great choice. There are so many delicious options available that once you have ditched the biscuits, you will never look back!

Guacamole Tartlets

Makes: **12**
Preparation time: **10 minutes**
Cooking time: **5 minutes**

Ingredients

- 2 large ripe avocados, halved and pitted
- 2 cloves of garlic, minced
- 2 limes, juiced
- 1 tsp hot sauce
- a small bunch of coriander (cilantro), chopped
- 12 small savoury tart shells
- 2 button mushrooms, sliced
- 1 stick of celery, peeled and thinly sliced
- ½ tsp Cayenne pepper
- salt and freshly ground black pepper

Method

1. Roughly chop the avocado flesh and add to a food processor along with the garlic, lime juice, hot sauce, most of the coriander and some seasoning.

2. Blitz the mixture until smooth, and adjust the seasoning to taste.

3. Spoon the smooth guacamole into the tart shells and arrange on serving plates.

4. Top with sliced mushroom and celery as well as a pinch of Cayenne and the remaining coriander as a garnish.

5. Serve immediately for best results.

Sweet Potato Crisps

Serves: **4**
Preparation time: **15–20 minutes**
Cooking time: **18–20 minutes**

Ingredients

- 2 medium sweet potatoes, peeled
- 2 tbsp sunflower oil
- ½ tsp paprika
- 1 tsp salt
- 2 tbsp desiccated coconut, to serve

Method

1. Preheat the oven to 160°C (140°C fan) / 325F / gas 3.

2. Thinly slice the sweet potatoes into very thin slices using a mandolin. Collect the slices in a large mixing bowl.

3. Pat the slices dry, then toss with the sunflower oil, paprika and salt.

4. Arrange the slices on two large baking trays, making sure they are in a single layer.

5. Bake for 18–22 minutes until the edges start to curl and the tops are dry.

6. Remove the trays to a wire racks to cool.

7. Once cool, serve with desiccated coconut on the side.

Roquefort and Walnut Crostini

Makes: **16**
Preparation time: **10 minutes**
Cooking time: **5 minutes**

Ingredients

- 4 slices of white sandwich bread
- 110 g / 4 oz piece of Roquefort
- 16 walnut halves
- 2 tbsp runny honey (optional)

Method

1. Toast the slices of bread in a toaster or under a hot grill until golden brown.

2. Remove from the grill and cut into quarters.

3. Cut the piece of Roquefort into small bite-sized chunks. Arrange on the toasts along with a walnut half.

4. Drizzle with honey (if using) before serving.

Mozzarella Balls

Serves: **8 as an appetiser**
Preparation time: **10 minutes**
Cooking time: **5 minutes**

Ingredients

- 8 slices of prosciutto
- 16 small fresh mozzarella balls, drained
- 110 ml / 4 fl. oz / ½ cup extra-virgin olive oil
- 75 g / 3 oz / ¾ cup shelled pistachios, crushed
- 16 wooden toothpicks
- a small handful of basil leaves
- salt and freshly ground black pepper

Method

1. Cut the slices of prosciutto in half. Dip the balls of mozzarella into the olive oil and then coat in the crushed pistachios.

2. Wrap in pieces of prosciutto and secure with a toothpick.

3. Cover and chill until ready to serve. Garnish with some basil leaves and a little salt and pepper.

Gluten-free Raisin Brioche

Serves: **8**
Preparation time: **1 ¾–2 ¼ hours**
Cooking time: **20–25 minutes**

Ingredients

- 250 g / 9 oz / 1 ⅔ cups gluten-free plain (all-purpose) flour
- 110 g / 4 oz / ½ cup unsalted butter, cold and cubed
- 1 ½ tbsp fast-action dried yeast
- a pinch of salt
- 3 medium eggs
- 150 g / 5 oz / 1 cup raisins
- 1 medium egg yolk, beaten

Method

1. Combine the flour and butter in a food process and pulse until it resembles fine breadcrumbs. Stir in the yeast and salt, then tip into a bowl.

2. Add the eggs and mix until a soft dough forms. Continue to knead for 4–5 minutes, then add the raisins and knead for a further minute.

3. Divide the dough into 8 and shape into balls, then drop into individual, lined moulds or ramekins. Cover loosely with oiled cling film and leave to rise in a warm place for 1 ½–2 hours or until doubled in size.

4. Preheat the oven to 190°C (170°C fan) / 375F / gas 5. Place the moulds on a baking tray and brush the tops of the dough with beaten egg yolk.

5. Bake for 20–25 minutes until golden on top and risen. Remove to wire racks to cool before serving.

Oat, Linseed and Flax Bars

Serves: **8**
Preparation time: **10 minutes**
Cooking time: **15–20 minutes**

Ingredients

- 300 g / 10 ½ oz / 2 cups rolled oats
- 2 tbsp flaxseeds
- 2 tbsp linseeds
- 150 g / 5 oz / ⅔ cup apple sauce
- 55 g / 2 oz / ¼ cup reduced-fat margarine
- a pinch of salt

Method

1. Preheat the oven to 180°C (160°C fan) / 350F / gas 4 and line a 18 cm (7 in) square baking tin with greaseproof paper.

2. Combine the oats, flaxseeds and linseeds in a large mixing bowl.

3. Melt together the apple sauce, margarine and salt in a pan set over a medium heat.

4. Whisk until smooth, then pour over the oats. Stir well to combine, then pack the mixture into the prepared tin.

5. Bake for 15–20 minutes until golden on top.

6. Remove the tin to a wire rack to cool completely, then turn out and cut into bars.

7. Serve immediately or store for up to three days in an airtight container.

Gluten-free Scones

Makes: **12**
Preparation time: **10 minutes**
Cooking time: **12–15 minutes**

Ingredients

- 55 g / 2 oz / ¼ cup butter, cold and cubed
- 225 g / 8 oz / 1 ½ cups gluten-free, self-raising flour, plus extra for dusting
- a pinch of salt
- 150 ml / 5 fl. oz / ⅔ cup semi-skimmed milk
- 1 small egg, beaten

Method

1. Preheat the oven to 190°C (170°C fan) / 375F / gas 5 and line a large baking tray with greaseproof paper.

2. Rub the butter into the flour and salt in a mixing bowl until the mixture resembles breadcrumbs.

3. Add the milk and mix well to form a soft dough.

4. Turn out the dough onto a lightly floured surface, pat into a round, and roll out to 2 cm (1 in) thickness. Use a 4–5 cm (2 in) round cutter to stamp out 12 rounds band arrange them on the tray.

5. Brush the tops with beaten egg and bake for 12–15 minutes until golden and risen.

6. Remove to a wire rack to cool completely before serving.

Chocolate Rice Cakes

Makes: **8**
Preparation time: **15 minutes**
Cooking time: **5 minutes**

Ingredients

- 150 g / 5 oz / 1 cup dark (90% cocoa) chocolate, chopped
- 8 plain rice cakes
- 2 tbsp desiccated coconut

Method

1. Place the chopped chocolate in a bain-marie set atop a saucepan of gently simmering water.

2. Stir occasionally until the chocolate has melted. Remove from the heat and leave to cool for 5 minutes.

3. Brush one side of the rice cakes with the melted chocolate using a pastry brush.

4. Sprinkle the tops of half with desiccated coconut. Leave the rice cakes to set on a wire rack before serving.

Puffed Rice Chocolate Bars

Serves: **8**
Preparation time:
2 hours 15 minutes
Cooking time: **5 minutes**

Ingredients

- 125 g / 4 ½ oz / 5 cups puffed rice
- 100 g / 3 ½ oz / ⅔ cup rolled oats
- 225 g / 8 oz / 1 ½ cups dark (90% cocoa) chocolate, chopped
- 55 g / 2 oz / ⅓ cup cocoa powder
- 55 ml / 2 fl. oz / ¼ cup semi-skimmed milk

Method

1. Grease and line an 20 cm (8 in) square baking tin with greaseproof paper.

2. Combine the puffed rice and oats in a large mixing bowl, then stir and set to one side.

3. Melt the chocolate in a bain-marie set atop a saucepan of simmering water.

4. Stir occasionally until the chocolate has melted. Remove from the heat and leave to cool slightly, then add to the rice and oats. Stir, then add the cocoa powder and milk.

5. Stir thoroughly until combined, then pack the mixture into the prepared baking tin.

6. Cover and chill for 2 hours until set.

7. Turn out the bar and cut into slices before serving.

No-sugar Financiers

Makes: **approximately 18**
Preparation time: **15 minutes**
Cooking time: **6–8 minutes**

Ingredients

- 125 g / 4 ½ oz / 1 ¼ cups ground almonds
- 3 small very ripe bananas, mashed
- 100 g / 3 ½ oz / ⅔ cup self-raising flour
- a pinch of salt
- 150 g / 5 oz / ⅔ cup reduced-fat margarine, melted
- 4 large egg whites
- powdered stevia for dusting

Method

1. Preheat the oven to 230°C (210°C fan) / 450F / gas 8 and grease two 12-hole financier moulds.

2. Combine the ground almonds, banana, flour and salt in a food processor. Blitz until smooth.

3. Add the egg whites and pulse until incorporated. Add the melted margarine and pulse again until a pourable batter forms.

4. Spoon the batter into the moulds and bake for 6–8 minutes until golden and risen.

5. Remove to a wire rack to cool completely before turning out and serving.

6. Dust with powdered stevia.

Flapjacks with Vanilla Topping

Serves: **8**
Preparation time: **15 minutes**
Cooking time: **20–25 minutes**

Ingredients

- 55 g / 2 oz / ¼ cup reduced-fat margarine
- 1 small banana, mashed
- 100 g / 3 ½ oz / ½ cup apple sauce
- 300 g / 10 ½ oz / 2 cups rolled oats
- 300 g / 10 ½ oz / 1 ½ cups low-fat cream cheese, softened
- 1 tsp vanilla extract

Method

1. Preheat the oven to 180°C (160°C fan) / 350F / gas 4. Grease and line an 18 cm (7 in) square baking tin with greaseproof paper.

2. Melt the butter in a saucepan set over a moderate heat. Pour into a food processor and blitz with the banana and apple sauce.

3. Scrape into a mixing bowl and add the oats. Mix thoroughly until combined.

4. Pack the mixture into the prepared tin, levelling the top with the back of a tablespoon. Bake for 20–25 minutes until golden on top before removing to a wire rack.

5. Once cool, beat the cream cheese with the vanilla extract until smooth. Turn out the flapjack and spread the top with the cream cheese before serving.

Popcorn and Nut Bars

Serves: **18**
Preparation time: **40 minutes**
Cooking time: **5 minutes**

Ingredients

- 125 g / 4 ½ oz / 12 cups plain popcorn (popped)
- 150 g / 5 oz / 1 cup rolled oats
- 75 g / 3 oz / ¾ cup walnuts, chopped
- 100 g / 3 ½ oz / ⅔ cup raisins
- 2 tbsp almonds, chopped
- 2 tbsp Brazil nuts, chopped
- ¾ tsp ground cinnamon
- 175 g / 6 oz / ¾ cup reduced-fat margarine

Method

1. Grease and line the base and sides of two rectangular 32 cm x 18 cm (13 in x 7 in) cake tins with greaseproof paper.

2. Combine the popped popcorn, rolled oats, walnuts, raisins, almonds, Brazil nuts and ground cinnamon in a large mixing bowl.

3. Melt the margarine in a saucepan set over a low heat. Once melted, leave to cool slightly and pour over the popcorn.

4. Mix well to coat thoroughly, then pack the mixture into the prepared tins. Make sure that the tops are flat and even using the back of a tablespoon.

5. Chill for at least 30 minutes before turning out, slicing, and serving.

Meal Plans and Diary

When starting a new diet, it is important to have a plan. Otherwise you will have a day – probably fairly early on – where you are pressed for time and don't have a menu planned or ingredients bought. It is at times like this when you are likely to reach for something comforting and familiar… and possibly full of sugar.

Before you start, sit down and think about how you want to tackle going sugar free. How far do you want to reduce your sugar intake each week? You should have a plan for how many grams of sugar you are allowed as you gradually cut it out of your diet. Also, jot down some targets for exercise and weight loss. It may seem like a lot to think about, but once you get into the swing of things, it will all become second nature.

In this chapter, you can plan and track your progress for six weeks. The first
three weeks have meal suggestions provided from the recipes in this book. After
that, it is up to you – you can mix and match the same recipes, or search for new
ones. The ideas and recipes in this book are only the tip of the iceberg as far as
delicious sugar-free food is concerned!

Once you have your plan in place and your shopping list written, make sure
to keep a record of everything you eat and drink. That way you cannot just
'forget' about that biscuit with your tea or soft drink or glass of wine at a friend's.
Before you know it, you will be sugar free!

Week 1

	Breakfast	Lunch	Snack	Dinner
Monday				
Tuesday				
Wednesday				
Thursday				
Friday				
Saturday				
Sunday				

Starting weight

Finishing weight

How I feel

Exercise log

Week 2

	Breakfast	Lunch	Snack	Dinner
Monday				
Tuesday				
Wednesday				
Thursday				
Friday				
Saturday				
Sunday				

Starting weight

Finishing weight

How I feel

Exercise log

Week 3

	Breakfast	Lunch	Snack	Dinner
Monday				
Tuesday				
Wednesday				
Thursday				
Friday				
Saturday				
Sunday				

Starting weight

Finishing weight

How I feel

Exercise log

Week 4

	Breakfast	Lunch	Snack	Dinner
Monday				
Tuesday				
Wednesday				
Thursday				
Friday				
Saturday				
Sunday				

Starting weight

Finishing weight

How I feel

Exercise log

Week 5

	Breakfast	Lunch	Snack	Dinner
Monday				
Tuesday				
Wednesday				
Thursday				
Friday				
Saturday				
Sunday				

Starting weight

Finishing weight

How I feel

Exercise log

Week 6

	Breakfast	Lunch	Snack	Dinner
Monday				
Tuesday				
Wednesday				
Thursday				
Friday				
Saturday				
Sunday				

Starting weight

Finishing weight

How I feel

Exercise log

Week 7

	Breakfast	Lunch	Snack	Dinner
Monday				
Tuesday				
Wednesday				
Thursday				
Friday				
Saturday				
Sunday				

Starting weight

Finishing weight

How I feel

Exercise log

Week 8

	Breakfast	Lunch	Snack	Dinner
Monday				
Tuesday				
Wednesday				
Thursday				
Friday				
Saturday				
Sunday				

Starting weight

Finishing weight

How I feel

Exercise log

Keeping It Off

Congratulations – you've done it! You've stuck to the sugar-free diet and are feeling the benefits already. You have more energy, you feel great, and you have lost some weight. Now comes the hard part: keeping it off. Many dieters reach their target and then lose the momentum to stick with the new routine. Here are a few tips for keeping motivated:

- Remember why you did it! Have a look at an old photograph of yourself and think about how you felt before you cut out sugar. Keep that old photo handy for whenever you have a craving or are feeling low
- If you have gone down a dress size, then clear out some of your old clothes, and treat yourself to a few things in your new size
- Set a new target. For example, now that you are healthier and fitter, maybe you could train for a fun run or even a half marathon. Keeping focused on goals can help keep you from backtracking

- Keep track. Weigh yourself once a week and give yourself a pat on the back every time you maintain your target weight
- Set an example. Your friends and family will notice how much better you are looking and feeling. Helping someone else to cut out sugar can keep you motivated to stick with it yourself

If you have cut out sugar entirely and are still craving a few favourite sweet treats even after months of sticking to your diet, then there is no harm in reintroducing it in small amounts. As long as you stay well within the recommended guidelines, an occasional small treat will not hurt. If you have stuck to the sugar-free diet then you know you have the willpower to keep your sugar intake under control. Moderation is the key!

Notes

Notes

Notes

Notes

Diet consultant: Jo Stimpson.

Main food photography and recipe development: PhotoCuisine UK.

All other recipe images courtesy of Thinkstock, Getty Images.

Cover: main idildemir/iStock; other PhotoCuisine UK.

Flap: PhotoCuisine UK.

Picture Credits
4 Dmitri Mihhailov/Shutterstock; 6 Matej Kastelic/ Shutterstock; 7 saurabhpbhoyar/Shutterstock; 8 picsfive/Shutterstock; 9 markos86/Shutterstock; 10t Elena Schweitzer/Dreamstime; 10b Jocic / Dreamstime; 11 Richard Thomas/Dreamstime; 12 Africa Studio/Shutterstock; 13 Warren Goldswain/ iStock; 14 Peter Bernik/Shutterstock; 15 B. and E. Dudzinscy/Shutterstock; 16 Steigele /Dreamstime; 18 Monkey Business Images/Dreamstime; 19 Stephen Mcsweeny/Shutterstock; 20 Alejandro Salvador Mir/iStock; 21 Kladej/Shutterstock, 22 Legaa/Dreamstime; 23 Ildipapp/Dreamstime; Paul Maguire/Dreamstime; 25 Goran Bogicevic/ Dreamstime; 26 Monkey Business Images / Shutterock; 27 Darren Baker/Dreamstime; 28 Andrey Arkusha/Shutterstock; 29 Aleksi/Shutterstock; 30 Diana Valujeva /Dreamstime; 31 tmcphotos/ Dreamstime; 32 Gavran333/Shutterstock; 33 Golyak/ Dreamstime; 168 Photographerlondon/Dreamstime; 169 B. and E. Dudzinscy/Shutterstock; 170 jf123/ Dreamstime; 171 Anna Sedneva/Shutterstock; 172 Marazen/Dreamstime; 173 Mariusz Blach/ Dreamstime; 174 Mohaned Osama/Dreamstime; 175 Dionisvera /Shutterstock; 176 Alexander Pladdet/ Dreamstime; 177 Alexstar/Dreamstime; 178 Maks Narodenko/Shutterstock; 179 Elovich/Shutterstock; 180 Duskbabe/Dreamstime; 181 Roman Samokhin/ Dreamstime; 186 aaron belford/Shutterstock; 187 Ariwasabi/Dreamstime; 192 Warren Goldswain/ Shutterstock.